Surface Decoration
for CERAMICS

a CREATIVE GUIDE for the CONTEMPORARY MAKER

Claire Ireland

Surface Decoration for CERAMICS

a CREATIVE GUIDE for the CONTEMPORARY MAKER

THE CROWOOD PRESS

CONTENTS

INTRODUCTION

Decorating a ceramic surface can be the most rewarding aspect of working in clay. This book is for the potter who wants to be more creative, more adventurous, to explore decorative techniques and have the chance to play. This is an opportunity to discover alternative and contemporary approaches to making marks on clay. It is intended to inform and inspire the maker, the student and the enthusiast, who are working at different levels and promoting a more experimental approach. I want to encourage a practice of testing, documenting and building a visual repertoire of surface techniques. There will be decorative methods that may be familiar, but the aim is to delve deeper and shed new light on the potential of each process, with alternative ways of incorporating them on to a ceramic surface.

The images and demonstrations will illustrate how to apply them, but treat this as merely a starting point, the chance to interpret each technique and make them your own. Surface decoration can be intense, busy or detailed, but can also be subtle, simply creating a quality of surface that is pleasing and tactile. The methods of decoration and mark-making are a culmination of the many years teaching students of different ages at different levels, and through experiments for my own work. I have also contacted makers from all over the world, who have a passion for decorative techniques and have generously shared their discoveries.

I have always had a fascination for experimental ceramic processes and techniques, which has helped develop my teaching methods but has also informed my practice. Throughout my teaching career I have worked with students who would eagerly

A sophisticated way to apply paper stencils by potter Georgie Gardiner, who can achieve crisp, graphic detail in her pieces.

◀ Making constructed stamps can be very addictive, and the opportunity to use a variety of materials and found objects is very appealing.

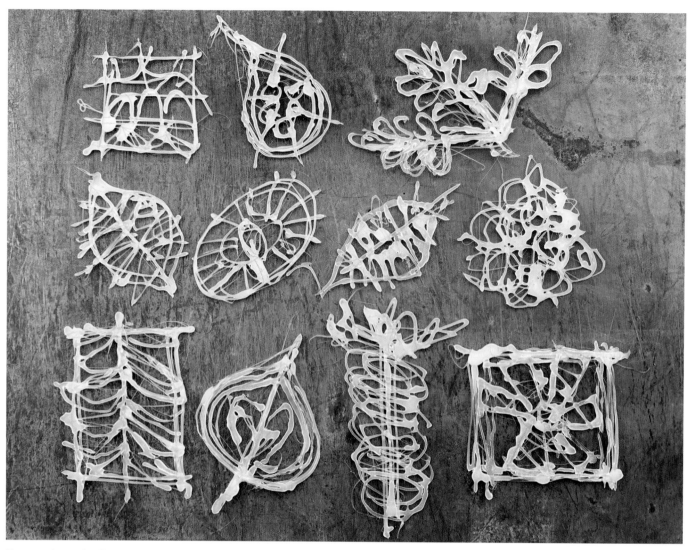

The meandering doodles made by a hot glue pen can produce detailed embossed linear marks when pressed into soft clay.

take up the challenge of creating a form in different ways, but would often struggle when it came to decorating the surface, and would find it rather daunting.

Developing a decorative surface can take as much time and effort as it does to create a ceramic form. However, it is crucial to take that extra time at this stage of the process. The embellishment of a piece can be the deciding factor for a successful outcome. So many ideas can come from decorative experiments and, more importantly, the mishaps. Creating a diversity of surfaces is a solid way to help to build up a body of work.

Experiment with as many techniques as you can – that is the fun part. Keeping a record of all your experiments is worthwhile, alongside a collection of small fragments and test pieces that will help to keep all that information fresh. It is so easy to miss those little gems. But beware: it can turn into a lifelong passion.

Fragments of dried, coloured china clay slip are embedded into a clay surface, using the American artist Mitch Lyon's inventive clay printing technique on a fabric substrate.

Embossed printed detail with underglaze colour and bespoke sterling silver fittings. Part of the author's Tension Visuelle collection of sculpture to wear.

Smoky graphic marks have been created using the fast-firing process, by applying paper stencils and clay slip to mask a biscuit fired surface.

CHAPTER 1

SKETCHBOOKS AND DESIGN

Making and drawing have always been important to me, and the two processes have become more entwined over the years. Drawing, alongside printmaking and collaging, has a crucial role in the development of my work. It is an activity that I take for granted, and is an integral part of my practice. It is also something I enjoy. Drawing can help find forms and make decisions regarding all aspects of making and decorating.

Reference is such an important factor of the whole process, but assembling a design vocabulary is just half of the story. Imagery that is inspiring will assist the building of resources in the shape of structures, patterns, texture and surfaces. The way to develop an approach to design, using any type of decoration, is through exploration and practice. Remember, drawing is not always about accuracy: one of its functions can be to get ideas out of your head and on to the page. Source material can also take the form of the written word, a story or poem, a sound or a scene in a film. These can be recorded as part of the research and developed into visual notations, or transcribed using collage or printmaking techniques, for example.

A sketchbook is an ideal place to start developing the sort of marks that can be made on the clay surface. Making versions of the patterns or textures on paper first can be a practice run, and the more information that is accumulated at the start, will give you the confidence to translate those ideas on to the clay.

SKETCHBOOKS: WHERE TO START

Ideas cannot be easily grasped out of thin air – they take time to develop, but it is a pleasant process. Grayson Perry, when enthusing about drawing, talks about 'becoming familiar with your voice on paper' (from the television series Channel 4 [first season] *Grayson's Art Club*, May 2020). He says about his approach: 'I draw as a collagist, juxtaposing images and styles of mark-making from many sources' (from *The Guardian and Observer Guide to Drawing*, September 2009).

Graffiti are often intended to be quite brash or edgy, but this tag engraved on to the glass at a bus-stop shelter has resulted in a more refined image.

◄ Inspiration can be found in the most unlikely places. Discovered in the garden of the museum, where the author's studio is based.

Inspiration can be absorbed from personal obsessions and different cultures. Subjects can range from the natural world, contemporary architecture, graffiti, ancient maps or folk art, for example. It is important to choose a subject that will keep you interested and help you to move forwards with the research.

Keep a sketchbook or small notebook to hand, and take it everywhere. Document gallery and museum visits, keeping a record of those special exhibitions. This can even include the tickets, the postcards and the photographs taken on your phone. Select the best images, maybe crop some of the detail and print them out, let them see the light of day. Any found fragments that are collected, as part of these journeys, can also be included.

I like to work on different scales in various sizes of sketchbook, from a square pocket-sized one, up to as large as A3, which, if using a double page, is 2ft (60cm) across. The larger books are more flexible if they are ring bound, and especially helpful if you want to add paper collage and found fragments to your pages, as I do.

Using different sorts of paper can change the outcome, such as a dense smooth paper, alongside tracing paper or sheets that have text on them. Sturdy envelopes provide a perfect surface for ideas. The artist Margaret Mellis, who made remarkable assemblages from found materials, also completed over seventy drawings on opened-out envelopes. The physical nature of their shapes dictated the design, often incorporating the printed patterns found on the inside of the envelope.

ALISON MILNER AND HER SKETCHBOOKS

Alison is passionate about research and has used the same type of A5 hardback sketchbook since 2005. She uses one about every six months, which works out about twenty pages a month. They are filled with copious notes and very loose diagrammatic-type drawings, with images that she has printed out, which document her work in progress. They are for her eyes only. She keeps them all together on a shelf and has thirty so far. They are not in any order, but she puts a small picture on the front of each one, which roughly indicates the time they were made. Crammed full of ideas, Alison refers to them constantly. This has progressed into an occasional series of continuous collages in concertina-style sketchbooks, which she refers to as 'streams of consciousness'.

She uses her large coffee table at home as a physical sketchbook, placing her ceramic components into different groups, using it to work through her ideas, often incorporating found objects and constantly rearranging them. Alison has always been a collector and an arranger of objects. She collects natural forms and simple man-made objects, which are mostly functional and usually made with one material and with processes she can understand. She rarely spends much money on her collections, and she likes the notion of her ceramics mingling unobtrusively with these objects. In her book *Inspirational Objects*, which is a visual dictionary of her collection, she explains that:

Alison's ideas sometimes progress into a series of continuous collages, presented in concertina-style sketchbooks, which she refers to as 'streams of consciousness'. (PHOTO: STEVE SPELLER)

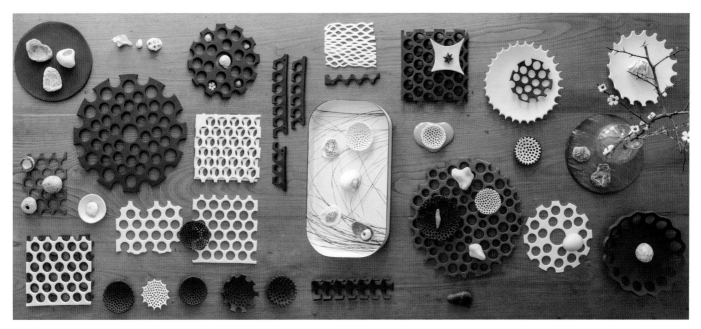

Work from part of the 'Nature Table' series. Alison Milner considers herself a collector and arranger of objects.
(PHOTO: STEVE SPELLER)

...the objects are arranged into a narrative, which only really exists in my mind; objects make connections with other objects, sometimes through their geometry, sometimes by their manufacture, and sometimes by their human associations.

Alison describes herself as a designer of '2D for 3D'. She has worked with a wide range of materials, having originally trained in furniture design. Learning about materials and extending processes through collaboration with other makers and manufacturers has been an essential part of her practice. After ten years of working with other ceramicists, she decided to make her own collection. She challenged herself to see how inventive she could be with two simple processes and three different clays. This project evolved into the 'Nature Table' ceramic collection.

She says of her work:

I like minimalism and patterns, the geometry of nature, slight imperfection, detail and space. I like things to have a place and belong to a group. I like to rescue mistakes and accept imperfections. I like fitness of purpose, improvisation and play, and I like to understand materials. I like 'looking'.

SKETCHBOOK DESIGN

Sketchbook Diaries

This approach to visual research resembles a diary, and some artists and makers prefer the narrative format of a journal, working on ideas on a regular basis. The flow of ideas is often interwoven into events of their everyday life. It can take the form of a scrapbook with fragments of mixed media, collage and text, or purely just drawings. Some will challenge themselves to contribute to a creative instalment every day. So often these hidden gems are used religiously by their owner, but so often are not shared with others. The artist Michael Craig-Martin wrote about his love of drawings and using sketchbooks, and remarked: 'They are the great secret of Art' (from 'Drawing the Line', South Bank Centre 1995: catalogue for a national touring exhibition of drawing selected by the artist).

Artist and maker Susan Coleman has kept a visual diary for about seven years, and uses it partly as a reminder of family events, but glimpses into her home life are intertwined with her ideas for her illustrative ceramics.

Drawings from Susan Coleman's diaries: her playful, illustrative style generates a continuous narrative about her life and the designs for her ceramics.

Themed Sketchbooks

I have often concentrated on specific subjects or themes for my sketchbooks and have developed this idea with students as a starting point for their projects. This disciplined approach can be very helpful as it can sharpen your observational skills and make you look more carefully. There is so much that we miss, and through these projects you can develop an interest in the obvious but often overlooked quality of things. Start by observing the hidden beauty in the natural and man-made environment.

Textures and Surfaces

Textures and surfaces make excellent subjects as there is an unlimited supply of options all around. Interesting textures are everywhere, and the more you look, the more you will find. These can be translated into drawings, rubbings, photographs, images from magazines and postcards. This can also include found fragments, samples of embossed or embroidered fabric, decorative paper, or even plastic packaging.

Take some care as to how to display them in your sketchbook. This decision-making is part of the creative process and may help to inform the ways this information is used. Cropping or editing an image can be a way to isolate the area that most interests you. Leave spaces on the page so that different versions can be made of the selections. Re-create them as a line drawing in ink, a monoprint, or a torn paper collage for example. Each time an image is reproduced, it can transform and develop, changing the proportions, reversing the image, or creating a repeat pattern.

Graphic Detail

Words and symbols can be found on almost every surface – on buildings, on shop windows, in layers of torn posters on old billboards and spray-painted graffiti on weathered walls. Road markings are a particular favourite of mine, and it is always a surprise that there are so many variations. Some have been worn over time and have often been renewed or repositioned, and have created some wonderful textural surfaces.

These temporary marks and symbols are known as utility traces, which are codes to denote the position of cables and pipes below the surface. These are often in different colours and can be very decorative. Architectural detail on buildings and pavements is another great source of graphic inspiration, and presents a wealth of information that would translate well into ideas for decoration.

Utility traces and road markings hold a particular fascination, and the patinas that develop over time are very enviable.

CRAIG UNDERHILL AND HIS USE OF SKETCHBOOKS

Craig is a maker with a fascination for graphic detail, and his textural and painterly approach is constantly influenced by his environment:

> I think I'm drawn to graffiti because I like the way it pushes the shape of letters to an extreme so they become almost unrecognizable. It's also the human intervention in the landscape that interests me, as well as the inevitable richness that is built up over time as images are applied over each other, while the effect of time causes constant, slow erosion. I like the shape and texture of writing rather than what it says.

He was introduced to the process of using sketchbooks while studying Ceramics at Harrow, and still has the thirty or so sketchbooks completed during that time; furthermore his visual research has remained a vital part of his working process today. He now works in larger sketchbooks, A3 size, which he uses to explore ideas, solve visual problems, and experiment with composition. It gives him the freedom to acknowledge that there is no wrong answer, or any specific way of doing something. He says of this process:

> My sketchbook is a place to take risks, and the discoveries that come from this help me to direct and make progress with my work. I feel I can work in a non-precious and more spontaneous way in my sketchbook, and this frame of mind is critical if artistic progress is to be made. My sketchbooks are also a place to experiment with unfamiliar materials and techniques to create visual imagery that could feed into or be adapted to work with ceramic materials.

The wealth of information that Craig has produced in his sketchbooks over three decades is vast – and these sketchbooks are still important to him and serve as an invaluable source of reference. Looking back through his sketchbooks he finds they serve as a diary of his ideas, thoughts and experiences.

Craig Underhill's sketchbooks are of prime importance to him, and a place where he can take risks and make discoveries.

A detail of one of Craig Underhill's painterly vessels that explores the same elements he aspires to in his sketchbooks.

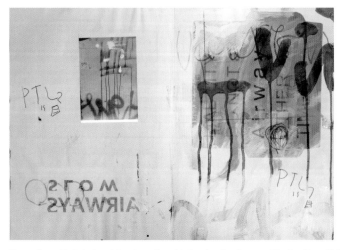

Pages from Craig's sketchbooks reflect his fascination for graphic detail, and his experiments with unfamiliar materials and techniques.

Found Objects

Collecting seems to be implanted into every artist's DNA, regardless of their discipline. The objects can be natural or man-made, and have been discovered and kept because of some fundamental interest the artist sees in them. They are used for inspiration – it may be that they have a tactile surface or an unusual shape that is so alluring it could be cast, used as a maquette, or pressed into soft clay. Sometimes an object is just so appealing that having it there in the collection can be the only reason.

Collecting can be an important part of a maker's research because they consider such objects to be essential to their ideas and methods of making – an integral part of their practice. How they collate, store, or even display these items is often a key element of their whole creative practice.

The author's collection of her favourite feathers, with a string of shell and sea-glass fragments, which are pinned up on her studio wall.

Vintage fishing floats are another of the author's passions, and she collects them for the winning combination of inspiring forms and tactile, colourful surfaces.

Alison Milner's 'Imaginary Tile Company' collection epitomizes the allure of found objects, and her skill in placing and presenting the fragments. (PHOTO: STEVE SPELLER)

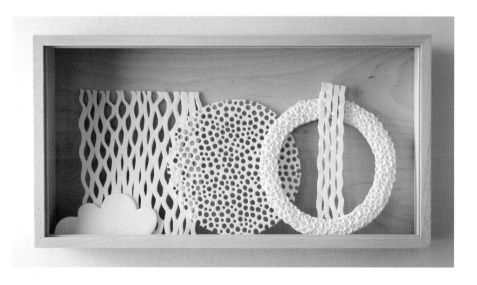

Ancient tools and fragments of machinery have wonderful sculptural qualities, the metal surface having the ability to develop rich patinas over time.

A selection of the fragments that the author displays on a shelf in her studio, and which serve as a constant narrative to her visual research.

SARAH RAYNER AND HER USE OF SKETCHBOOKS

Sarah lives in the Australian bush on the hinterland of the Sunshine Coast. From there she collects small specimens of interest: tiny things that draw her in and require close observation, mostly seedpods and tiny native flowers. She is drawn to the understated and often overlooked objects in hidden spaces and places. This micro view leads to a fascinating world of intricacy and complexity. Sarah says of her collections:

Sarah Rayner in her studio, sorting and collating plant fragments and seed pods; this is a crucial part of her creative practice. (PHOTO: FLORE VALLERY-RADOT)

I'm inspired by the sheer ingenuity and tenacity of plants and the clever methods they have evolved to attract pollinators. Of particular interest are the reproductive organs, primarily the Gynoecium, a collective term for the parts of a flower that produce ovules and ultimately develop into the fruit and seeds. I scrutinize and dissect these amazing little structures, examining the form, textures, cracks and crevices, and the way layers peel back to reveal sensuous interiors.

This process of collecting and collating Australian native seed-pods and flowers is a crucial aspect of Sarah's practice. Each week she arranges fresh native flowers she has picked from her garden and displays them in small glass bottles on her work desk to observe them closely and admire them.

She has a huge collection of seedpods in varying stages of maturity. Some are picked during the very early stages of development, whilst others are fully matured. Seeing how they grow, watching the varying stages of development and the way they harden, twist and burst open, she finds inspirational. She regularly arranges a selection of seedpods, experimenting with their relationships to one another, through shape and form, and creating a new order and dialogue. She considers it a taxonomy with no scientific basis; it is a form of play, of research and observation integral to her practice.

Drawing the seedpods is an important part of the process. The sketches are not realistic representations: they document specific features, preliminary ideas and translations of her observations and research. She edits the essential shapes and characteristics of multiple pods, often merging them into hybrid forms.

Her research flourishes into three-dimensional ceramic sculptures possessing aspects of plant life, which are simultaneously familiar yet strange, real and imagined. Sarah says of her porcelain pieces 'Many layers of musing are stored inside these little objects; sometimes they are sealed up and other times little bits are revealed.'

Sarah regularly arranges small posies of the native flowers collected from her garden, to display, observe and record at her work desk.

Sarah's renditions of these hybrid organic forms are part real, part imagined plant life, and they emerge as intricate porcelain structures.

Drawing the seedpods is an important part of the process for Sarah, and translating them into creative plant forms with porcelain. (PHOTO: GREG PIPER)

CATHERINE WHITE'S SKETCHBOOKS

Catherine White lives and works in Warrington, Virginia, located just forty-seven miles from Washington DC. She is an experienced maker with a long-standing career working with clay, which is inexorably woven into a daily practice of painting and drawing. She is constantly seeking a poetic language of material, shape and surface. Her work makes references to the landscape in an abstract way, through the raw materials she collects and her experiments with clay bodies and firing techniques. Catherine explains the importance of this approach:

> My sketchbooks are how I process my life. They are nets that catch my experiences, images, thoughts and ideas. I have different styles of books for distinct aspects of my work. I have a letter-sized book in which I alternate a page of longhand writing with an image page.

Catherine works in these sketchbooks five days a week and considers them 'a confidant'. She explores her ideas or 'spews out her emotions'. They are rough and ready, not intended for anyone else to see.

> Then I have a book that is strictly images, that accumulates collaged drawings. Each page starts with a coat of colour; facing pages are often mirrored, although different. On some painted pages I practise brushwork or experimental mark-making.

Catherine developed a method of mixing acrylic paint with methylcellulose, so the paint would mimic how she works with clay slips. This way she can effectively explore ideas on paper before she commits to clay. Ultimately the image books are bulging, the pages all pasted together into a wonderful fat mess. Catherine often cuts up pages and glues them in as backgrounds for imagined plates and bowls. Through this cutting and pasting of paper, she realized that she loved it when the marks moved off the page. So she began working with clay sizes larger than the desired final size, so she could initially draw beyond the frame. By cropping after completing the drawing, she achieved a fluid quality to the mark-making.

The final three notebooks she uses are more technical. She has a clay notebook where she records what she is making, documenting weights, shapes, and sizes of wet work. Then if she needs to remake something or shift dimensions, she

A detail from one of Catherine White's collaged sketchbooks, where she practises brushwork and experimental mark making.

Catherine constantly explores her ideas on paper, often cutting up and gluing together collaged fragments before she commits the design to clay.

has a record of where she started. With a shrinkage rate of almost 15 per cent with the processes she uses, this has proved helpful. In the studio she shares with her husband and fellow maker Warren Frederick, there is a clay notebook with clay body recipes, a slip and glaze notebook that records all their material combinations so they can choose to duplicate or adjust as desired. Details of Catherine's decorative technique using raw materials are featured in Chapter 5.

Drawing, painting and keeping sketchbooks are integral components to Catherine White's work as a potter, and are part of her daily studio practice. (PHOTO: WARREN FREDERICK)

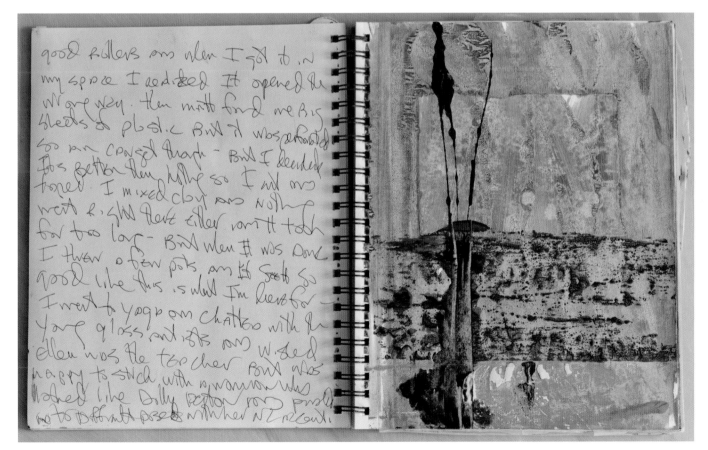

A glimpse into the sketchbooks that Catherine calls her 'confidant', where she explores her ideas and lets her emotions flow on to the page. (PHOTO: WARREN FREDERICK)

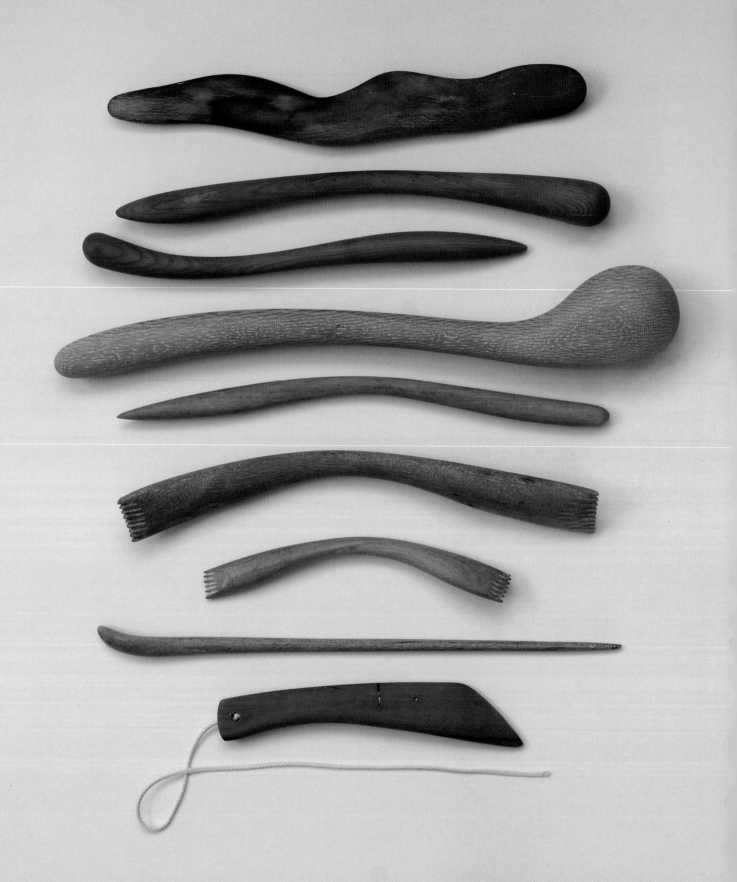

CHAPTER 2

TOOLS AND EQUIPMENT

Potters are passionate about their tools, and many makers have created and developed their own personal collections over time. Some of the most useful implements can be the ones used for creating a surface decoration, and the right kind of tool can make all the difference. There is an abundance of tools and objects that can be used to create a variety of marks and embellishments on the clay surface. Some will be multi-functional and can be used across all the making methods. This is something that evolves as each maker chooses which creative path to take.

There has been a long tradition for potters to improvise when making their own tools, often from found objects or even adapting a tool that was designed for another function. My list is based on my ceramic practice and the sort of tools I use most days, including ones I think will be relevant to the types of techniques explored in this book. It may seem like a long list, but keep in mind it should only act as a guide. Tools are very personal to the individual maker, often dictated by the methods they choose to explore. Feel free to amend, adapt and introduce your own personal favourites.

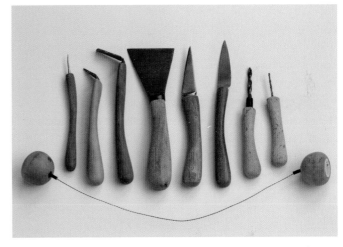

Chris Weaver's passion for making his own tools over the years has developed into a practical and enviable collection.

ESSENTIAL TOOLS AND ITEMS

Brushes

One of the most essential items, brushes can be used at different stages of making and for an array of decorative techniques. It is useful to have an assortment of sizes and shapes at your

Brushes are an essential part of any potter's tool kit, and having a variety of shapes and sizes will cover an array of practical and decorative tasks.

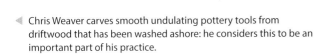
Chris Weaver carves smooth undulating pottery tools from driftwood that has been washed ashore: he considers this to be an important part of his practice.

disposal. There is a huge range available, so be selective, as they can be expensive. The style of brushes chosen will depend on the type of work, and what tasks are required. The ones I find most useful are a mop-head brush, flat lacquer brushes of different sizes, and a range of pointed wash brushes. Another way to explore more experimental marks is to make your own brushes, which is explained in detail in Chapter 4.

Knives

A thin-bladed precision knife such as a scalpel is the type I find to be the most useful. The replaceable blades ensure it stays sharp and precise. There is a variety of potter's knives that have a tapered blade, available from ceramic suppliers. Another alternative is to sharpen a section of a hacksaw blade to create a sharp-angled edge, which can be resharpened and has the bonus of a serrated section. This resembles a Kiridashi knife, which I have recently discovered and enjoy using: it is a traditional wood-carving knife that is widely used in Japan, 'kiridashi' meaning 'to carve out'. It has a sharp blade and is often used as an all-purpose utility knife.

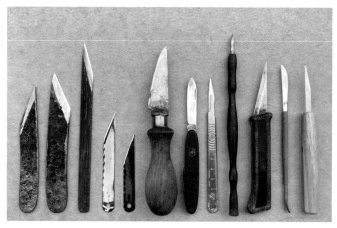

Potter's knives can take on different forms, often adapted from other tools. The Kiridashi-style craft knives, far left, are a new addition.

Plaster Blocks

Casting blocks of plaster in different sizes will prove to be invaluable, and ideal for creating different printing techniques. Most of the projects will require one or more panels, and they should be no smaller than A4 – but often a larger panel will allow more freedom. If there is space available, it is worth casting a generous block up to 2ft (61cm) square. Details about mixing plaster and casting blocks are fully explained in Chapter 5.

Silicone Ribs

Ribs are a very useful tool and come in different shapes and sizes, and ranges of flexibility. They are great for smoothing, but prove very effective when it comes to decorating; they are more durable and versatile than the traditional rubber kidney.

Stainless Steel Ribs

These metal ribs also come in varying degrees of flexibility and different shapes, but some are available with micro-fine teeth, which allows the maker to do detailed finishing.

Plastic Credit Cards

Many companies issue plastic cards now, and as these expire they become a great resource for the potter. They can be used just like a rib, but the added advantage is that they can be easily cut and adjusted to any size or shape for specific tasks.

Silicone and stainless-steel ribs are available in different shapes and in a range of flexibility; they are often the most frequently used tools.

Plastic cards are readily available and have the advantage of being flexible enough to be cut with scissors and adapted for stencils and shaping edges.

Pony Roller

This dual hardwood roller is used for flattening or smoothing clay and is the perfect tool to use with the slip transfer techniques. They are available through most ceramic suppliers, but catering companies have identical versions that are used for rolling out pastry and pizza dough.

Rolling Pins and Wooden Guides

I use a variety of sizes, so it is useful to have a larger one, a regular size and a mini one, when dealing with smaller fragments of clay. Roller guides can be used to control the thickness of the clay, and wooden battening works well; they are available in different thicknesses from builder's merchants.

Mallets and Paddles

These wooden tools are a simple solution to shaping, forming and compressing clay, and most potters will have a selection in their tool kit. Although there is a variety available from pottery suppliers, vintage plumber's tools and wooden spatulas designed for the kitchen are among the alternative versions that potters prefer to use.

Rolling Out Cloth or Board

Use a smooth but heavy-duty fabric to roll out clay, as it will prevent it from becoming creased as it starts to get damp. I also use panels of chipboard, as the clay does not stick to this surface, and it helps to dry the rolled-out clay evenly.

Sponges

A standard washing-up sponge is very versatile: it can be used to improve a ceramic surface, but can easily be cut into shapes for stamps. The most effective type has a heavy-duty green scourer over one side, which can be used to distress a surface. A range of smooth finishing sponges and natural sea sponges are available from ceramic suppliers and can be used for more delicate tasks.

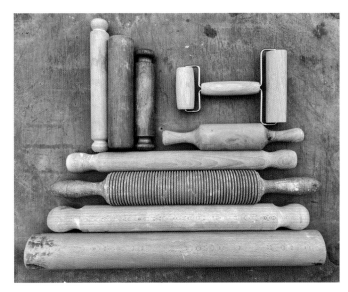

Another essential item for the dedicated hand builder; having a variety of rolling pins in different sizes should cover all requirements.

Vintage plumber's tools, mallets, domestic wooden spatulas and spoons are a popular choice among potters.

Sponges are another important part of a potter's kit; while some are ideal for creating sponge stamps, others can be used to smooth and refine a surface.

Sgraffito and Stylus Tools

These precision tools are available through ceramic suppliers, and can be purchased in sets. They have a precise cutting edge and can be used to sculpt, engrave and incise detail. Found objects such as drill bits, large nails, a compass or a large darning needle can be useful substitutes.

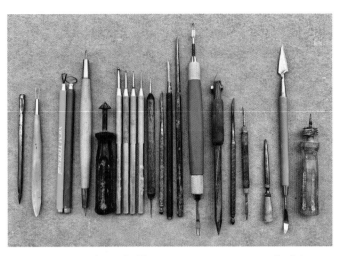

These engraving tools are ideal for intricate carving, cutting and refining detail, having the ability to create a variety of marks.

Modelling tools are not only pleasant to use, but come in a vast array of shapes and sizes; found wooden fragments can also be added into the mix.

Wooden Modelling Tools

These are one of the most comforting tools to use. Certain shapes I use constantly, and they improve with age, with the wood wearing slightly – they are a pleasure to handle. I will often sand the end if they have started to change shape through constant use. I will often improvise with found fragments of wood, which is often dictated by a certain task or mark I am trying to achieve.

Chris Weaver's Modelling Tools

Chris Weaver is one of New Zealand's most accomplished makers of tableware, and has built his studio and kilns on the remote west coast of South Island where he lives, which is rich in natural resources and scenic beauty. A skilled carpenter, Chris makes his own modelling tools with driftwood, and fabricates sturdy curved handles from Kiwi hardwood for his

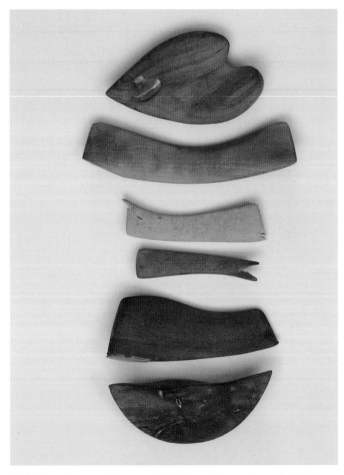

Chris Weaver has carved fragments of driftwood to create very tactile ribs, which have developed a patina with use.

Chris Weaver has extended his wood-making skills to create exquisitely made curved handles for his faceted teapots.

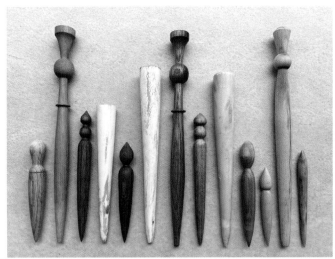

These tactile wooden tools are used to shape and make teapot spouts; their tapered forms can also make perfectly neat holes in different sizes.

jars, dishes and teapots. He takes time and great care in making the handles and the tools, as they are an important part of his practice: 'I find driftwood to make my own tools from the wood that has been swept down the flooded rivers and washed up on local beaches. I use these tools not as replacement for, but as an extension of my fingers, and they allow me to do more.' The shapes are dictated by the wood itself, following the grain and the natural washed, worn kinks in the wood.

Wooden Spout and Hole Makers

I have discovered different types of this tapered wooden tool, designed for other purposes, as they resemble a garden dibber used for sowing seeds and a spurtle, a Scottish kitchen tool used for stirring soups and porridge. They are such pleasing shapes, and although there are versions that can be bought from a potter's supplies, I often look to specialist makers for a more personal approach – I have recently worked with a woodworking team based in Scotland (details of Slate Road Designs can be found in the list of specialist contributors).

Serrated tools are yet another useful addition to a potter's toolkit, as not only can they be used in a variety of decorating techniques, but they are also useful tools in the making process.

Serrated Tools

Serrated tools can be used for a variety of tasks as they come in different shapes and are available in wood, metal or plastic, making them very versatile. They are ideal for scoring, scraping, texturing, refining, shaping and removing clay.

Kristina Riska's Humble Tools

Kristina Riska is one of Scandinavia's foremost contemporary ceramic artists and a senior member of the Arabia Art Department Society in Helsinki. She creates large-scale, ethereal vessels, inspired by nature and the properties of light and shadow, which embody her rigorous and physical approach to her work. She has a fascination for tools, and the simple domestic fork features heavily in her collection – she uses it to create her surfaces, as different forks give different effects.

She explains: 'From New York I bought an oyster fork, which has three very sharp teeth and can draw a deep line. Old silver forks have very thin tines and the trail is narrow and delicate. It is a pity that clay eats away silver, so I very seldom use silver forks.'

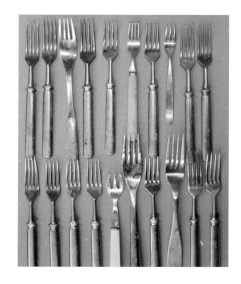

Kristina Riska's 'special tools', as she calls them, are a collection of domestic forks, which she uses to engrave the surface. (PHOTO: RIIKKA FRIMAN)

A detail of the textured surface, created with the humble fork, on one of Kristina Riska's large, hand-built forms.

A glimpse into Kristina Riska's studio. She works on a large scale and hand builds the forms slowly and meticulously, creating the surface as she goes.

Kristina refers to these templates as 'Precious Tools', made in high fired porcelain clay, used to create impressions into the clay surface. (PHOTO: RIIKKA FRIMAN)

Kristina Riska at work on one of her large, otherworldly vessels, creating the surface as she builds the form. (PHOTO: REA BRUNILA)

'While travelling I always try to find a hardware store or an artist's accessory shop. I love tools, and I always carry my favourite ones with me if I travel somewhere to work.' Kristina's studio is in an old porcelain factory – the factory is now closed, but when she first arrived, production was in full swing. 'They had a tradition of making tools for different stages of their ceramic process. Knives from saw blades, rubber rings from tyres, and I still use the knives.' The first tool she made was a wooden hammer when she was working towards her Master's thesis. She considers a wooden spatula a good tool, especially if it is covered with a soft, thick sock.

The first template Kristina made for cutting holes into the clay was made from plastic and was square in shape. When she wanted to make the holes round or organic, she made the 'sablons' from porcelain clay.

After getting tired of cutting holes into the clay walls, she discovered that pressing clay through the shapes she was able to achieve a more interesting effect on the surface. 'Today,' she says, 'many years later, I have hundreds of porcelain templates, "sablons" in different shapes. They are fired as high as possible and I have them attached to a fishing line around my neck to prevent them falling to the floor, as they will break immediately.'

Surform Blades

This tool was designed to work on wood by shaving thin slivers from the surface to shape the form. It resembles a food grater, but is made of steel, with each hole having a cutting edge. Potters have adopted it as an integral part of their tool kit, as it proves to be a popular choice to control and shape a surface evenly. The most effective one comes with a handle and a replaceable curved blade.

Slip Trailers

Precision slip-trailing kits come in a variety of shapes – some have screw tops and there is a selection of different precision nozzles. These work well, and prevent the slip from spurting out while being used. Small plastic squeezy bottles used in the catering industry are a great alternative, and can be adapted to create finer lines.

The trailing kits and applicators allow for more flexibility, are easier to use, and the precision tips can produce unique effects with detailed and fluid designs.

Mark Dally's Slip-Trailed Decoration

Mark Dally is a ceramic artist who specializes in slip-trailed decoration. He has developed and marketed his own version, after many years of experimenting with different trailers, unable to find one that achieved the consistency he required. (More details about his slip trailer can be found in the specialist suppliers' section.)

Working from his Staffordshire studio, Mark makes his Black & White Ware in high-fired white earthenware – his tableware includes teapots, mugs, jugs, platters and bowls. He decorates by slip trailing and brushing black and white slips on to paper resist cutouts, layered with slipped dots, drips and linework. He mixes his slip into a thick cream with about 11 per cent stain, and uses a 150-mesh sieve to achieve a smooth, refined mixture for trailing. For his stencil work, Mark uses a carnival paper, which retains its strength when wet and is designed for sculpting, lantern making and parade structures.

An initial training in textiles, and a passion for pattern and design, has influenced his approach to ceramic decoration. He explains that other inspirations…

…come from seventeenth-century Staffordshire slip trailing, mid-century Stoke-on-Trent industrial ceramics such as 'Homemaker' by Ridgway and Carlton Ware 'Walking Ware', and the sci-fi anachronisms of the 1940s, 1950s and 1960s animations and comics. I like to combine traditional craft and contemporary techniques in a modern take on Staffordshire slipware and flatbacks.

Sieves and Lawns

A wooden sieve with an 80-mesh size is a good choice, and is an essential item for the studio when preparing slips and glazes. The smaller plastic cup lawns or test sieves are ideal for smaller batches and preparing colours. In some of the techniques, domestic sieves are ideal for casting slip and making dust prints with powdered clay or pigment.

A large platter by designer maker Mark Dally, who is a skilful slip trailer and has developed and manufactured his own slip trailer.

Hand-held graters and small domestic sieves are the ideal tool to create coloured clay dust and fragments for different printing techniques.

Graters

Domestic food graters, mini sieves or tea strainers are ideal for using with dried sticks of stained clay or leather-hard blocks of coloured slip to create dust and small shavings of colour for several printing techniques.

Containers

Bowls, jugs and small containers are vital for all aspects of the making. If some of the small tubs have fitted lids, they can be used to store dry materials, prepared slips, colours or glazes.

Boards

Smooth plywood boards are perfect for supporting work throughout the different stages of making and drying. Builder's merchants and woodyards will often have offcuts that are ideal for this purpose. Sections of cement board are a practical and alternative surface to lay out sheets of clay. This is a combination of cement and reinforcing fibres formed into sheets of varying thickness that are typically used as a tile backing board and are water-resistant and not prone to warping.

Ceramic Tiles

Glazed tiles are a versatile part of the studio equipment. They can be used as a palette for mixing colours and oxides or emergency batches of slurry. They can be used as a printing plate, as it is easy to control the amount of pigment, when achieving a precision print. There are always a few spare tiles left over from recent DIY projects, but local suppliers will often have the basic white or discontinued tiles available at a reasonable price.

Fine Mist Sprayer

Unlike a normal pump spray bottle, this type of sprayer can give a continuous fine mist spray, resulting in an even and consistent coverage; this is especially helpful for the printing and paper transfer techniques, and avoids saturating delicate surfaces.

MATERIALS AND TEXTURES

Stencils

Plastic stencils can be obtained commercially and are usually aimed at the scrapbooking market. Stencils can be hand cut with a heated stencil cutter using polyester stencil sheets, or they can be made from paper and thin card using a sharp scalpel or craft knife. Digital cutting machines using wireless technology can translate drawings into stencils on a variety of materials including vinyl, which works well on a fired ceramic surface.

Newsprint is the most popular option among potters for creating stencils. It is a high quality, lightweight recycled paper, used for working out ideas, designing drafts and printing proofs. It is very smooth, but strong enough to cope with a variety of decorative methods used by makers. There is a rough version of newsprint that is a bit more robust and a slightly heavier weight, which I prefer to use, but a smoother one will work just as well. Tyvek material is ideal for a more durable stencil, and can be used several times as it is made from high density polythene fibres. It is a non-woven material resembling paper, but it is lightweight and resistant to water, and is used in different industries for insulation, packaging, apparel, décor and design.

Textured and Embossed Paper

Textured wallpaper is an excellent way to start a collection of embossed paper. It can be obtained free as it is acceptable to take a section as a sample from major hardware stores. Suppliers usually have open rolls available for just that reason. The paper can be used directly on to the clay, or sections can be cast in plaster. Corrugated paper is another reliable source of embossed paper, and is widely available – collect different examples from packaging and take-away wrappings.

Commercial or handmade stencils in plastic and paper are an imaginative way to create graphic images in a variety of decorative methods.

Textured wallpaper is a valuable source of intricate and elaborate embossed designs that can be pressed into clay.

Corrugated cardboard can be varied in its design; it is a flexible paper to use, as the layers can be peeled, torn and distressed to adjust the surface.

Fabric

Crochet, knitted or lace fragments and heavily embroidered fabric can be an ideal way of embossing a clay surface; the fragments can also be cast in plaster. It is worth starting to make a collection sourced from family and friends, or searching in charity shops for good samples.

Starting a collection of embossed and embroidered textiles is worthwhile, as they can be very effective when pressed into soft clay.

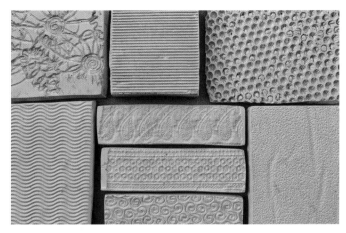

Casting sections of the textile or paper fragments in plaster can provide a permanent printing block for favourite textures.

MISCELLANEOUS TOOLS AND EQUIPMENT

Craft Knives

There are several craft cutting tools available that are ideal for stencil cutting and designed for precision cutting paper, card and vinyl. They work like a pen and have a rotating blade that can cut complex shapes with ease. These have more flexibility than a regular scalpel, but make sure the blades are sharp.

Exposure Board Kit

These panels make up the kit to create a simple and low-tech version of a silkscreen stencil using sunlight; they work well at A4 size – 21 × 29.7cm (8¼ × 11¾in).

- Felt back-board, using self-adhesive black felt fabric stuck to a rigid board
- Clear acrylic panel
- Heavy-duty cardboard panel
- Plastic canvas sheet
- Six bulldog clips

The additional materials required to make the silkscreen stencil are a pre-coated emulsion stencil film, the transparent film used for a laser printer, and a hi-opaque extra-fine black marker. (Details on this process can be found in Chapter 5.)

Rotary Tool

A rotary tool is a small, hand-held device with a rapidly spinning motor tip designed to accept a wide range of bits and

Using an exposure board kit is a simple, low-tech way to create a silk screen printing stencil from personal designs, using natural sunlight.

attachments. This versatile tool can cut, grind, sand, drill and polish, which makes it perfect for a wide range of tasks throughout the ceramic process.

Soldering Iron

This is a useful tool to engrave sponge stamps, and the heated nib can cut into the sponge very easily with great flexibility to make intricate marks. It is more effective than the stencil cutter due to the size and variety of the nibs available. It is important that this is done outside, and a mask should be worn as the fumes are toxic.

Flexible Plaster Bowls

These are very flexible rubber bowls that come in different sizes. They are used for mixing and pouring plaster, as it is possible to squeeze them together quite easily to make a pouring spout. Due to their flexibility, any residue plaster that has set can be easily removed by manipulating the bowl.

Cottles

The most efficient method to enclose an object ready for casting in plaster is to use wooden boards, a sheet of flexible plastic, or sections of acrylic tubing, referred to as cottles. Clamps, clips or heavy-duty tape can be used to hold them together, and soft clay to seal the base or any gaps, preventing the plaster from leaking during the casting process. For smaller moulds, clay walls can be used, but these are not so practical for larger projects, due to the weight of the plaster.

Wet-and-Dry Sandpaper

An effective way to achieve a smooth, polished finish to a ceramic surface is to use fine grade abrasive paper. This can be achieved after it has been biscuit fired, as the surface is still quite soft. Wet-and-dry sandpaper is used with water as lubrication, and will help carry the grit particles that are being removed. A more robust material to use, which can also create decorative marks, is a net abrasive called Abranet. Its hook-and-loop design makes it more durable than most sandpapers, and it will last longer. (More details about its decorative uses can be found in Chapter 8.)

Sand-Blasted Glass

I have a couple of panels of sand-blasted glass in the studio: it has a gritty surface, and when lubricated with water can level surfaces and edges of ceramic structures at the leather-hard stage. The trick is to keep it wet enough to be able to glide the piece easily over the surface of the glass, as there is a risk of getting stuck mid-way through the process.

HEALTH AND SAFETY

We have chosen to work with a medium that is not without risks. Working safely is common sense when handling different materials and organizing the working environment, and some basic guidelines are a matter of good practice. It is important to manage and control the dust in the work area, and always to wear a mask when handling dry and powdered materials. Dust masks are designed to protect the wearer from inhaling airborne particles, which could be in the form of dust, mist or fumes. Inhaling such particles can affect your health, especially if certain tasks are carried out frequently, such as sanding or carving on very dry clay, mixing plaster or spraying glazes.

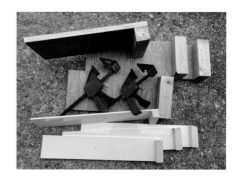

Cottles are the most practical way to create support walls for casting in plaster. These home-made versions can be clamped together and adjusted to any size.

Acrylic tubing can be used as a cottle when casting, and with different sizes available, is a practical way to create a neat plaster mould.

There are three different ratings for the masks: FFP1, FFP2 and FFP3 – these are governed by European standards, and each code is a step up and gives greater protection. For most tasks in the pottery, FFP1 or FFP2 masks would provide minimum and moderate levels of protection and are perfectly acceptable. However, if creating fumes by engraving and burning into sponge, it is advisable to use an FFP3 mask.

It is important to label bags of materials, colours and oxides with a permanent marker as paper labels tend to come off and so many ingredients look very similar. Label all prepared slips, colours and glazes on the lid and the side of the containers, and also give details of the recipe for future reference. Always close and seal bags and containers after use, and keep the working area clean, washing down surfaces and benches regularly – and this should include tools and any equipment used. Clean up spillages and wash hands after handling ceramic materials. Wear suitable overalls or an apron, and make sure they are washed regularly so they are not saturated with layers of dried materials. Have a clean towel to hand to wipe your hands or mop up spills, rather than wiping your hands on your apron.

CHAPTER 3

TEXTURE AND EMBOSSING

Clay is the ideal material to impress and create sculptural marks on the surface. There is no other material so receptive to texturing, and especially when at the soft malleable stage, it will retain any imprint you impose on it. Creating textures and making marks in clay has so many possibilities, and the scope for experimentation is endless. Stamped decoration has been widely used throughout the centuries, and is one of the earliest methods of making marks on pottery. There are several ways to make a stamp, which can be hand-made from a variety of different materials and then pressed into soft clay to create a texture, an impression, or a repeat pattern.

BISCUIT STAMPS

The ideal condition of the clay to make a stamp is when it is relatively soft, but not sticky, as it is vital to have a malleable surface to get the best results. Use a heavy-duty fabric (rolling-out cloth) or a panel of chipboard to roll out a thick sheet of clay. This can be achieved by stacking several wooden slats together, or use wooden blocks to get the desired thickness. Aim for about 4cm (1½in) in depth, which provides a generous layer to work with, and prepare several modest sheets, which will offer the freedom to experiment.

WHAT YOU WILL NEED

The following chapters will all have a list of materials and equipment as a guide for each set of techniques featured. For the stamps made of clay, I recommend using a white stoneware body, a grogged sculptural body, and a very smooth modelling clay.

Equipment
- Rolling out cloth or chipboard panel
- Rolling pin and wooden battens
- Small wooden blocks or thin panels of wood
- Wooden dowels
- Firm plastic rib
- Plastic card
- Paintbrushes
- Scalpel or potter's knife
- Sgraffito or engraving tools
- Hammer
- Flexible plaster mixing bowl
- A panel of thick glass or melamine-covered wood

Materials
- Collection of found objects, man-made and natural
- Wood glue
- Epoxy resin
- Masking tape
- Cardboard
- Small cardboard tubes
- Wine corks
- Thin cotton sheet (handkerchief size)
- Collage fragments and textured fabric
- Lace or crochet
- Embossed wallpaper samples
- String or wool
- Modelling paste
- White acrylic paint
- Talc
- PVA glue
- Plaster
- Wire, nails or tacks

◄ Roulettes made from fired clay and plaster, with a variety of different home-made handles that generate a continual band of decoration.

Using a smooth hand-building body for this method will achieve the best results, and is the perfect time to introduce some found objects and fragments into the process, and explore their potential as mark-making tools. Amongst my collection are bits of discarded jewellery, sea treasures, plastic fragments and metal oddments from the forge next door to my studio.

Making Pouncing Bags

If the items are not porous and are made of plastic, glass or metal, for example, they are likely to stick to the clay, so dusting the clay surface with talc will encourage a smooth release. I use baby talcum powder, which I place into a small fabric bundle, resembling a pouncing tool. This makes it much easier to distribute an even layer on to the clay surface. The powder is released when the bundle is tapped on to the clay using a dabbing action. The bundle can be made of a circle of fine muslin fabric, but I have found the panels from a disposable mask are ideal – this can be taken apart by cutting along each end where the elasticated loops are attached; there are three layers, but the two open-weave panels can be used. Place a couple of teaspoons of talc into the centre of each piece of fabric, then gather up the sides and bind them firmly together with a length of elastic cut from the mask. Another option is to cut the foot section from a pair of tights – the nylon mesh is stretchy enough to just tie the end into a knot after it has been filled with talc.

Collecting found fragments is in a maker's DNA, and a variety of materials will supply the potential for creating dynamic impressions on the clay surface.

Pouncing bags are easy to make and are an effective way to apply talc to a clay surface to prevent items sticking.

Making Biscuit Stamps Using Found Objects

This is an opportunity to raid your collection of found objects, collage fragments and sea treasures, using sections to press into soft clay and transforming them into embossed stamps.

Step 1: Press an array of found objects and fragments into the clay surface and see how they work.

Step 2: Try out different combinations, or repeat an image across the surface. Try pressing the texture through a fine cotton sheet or thin plastic film as this will produce a softer, more rounded impression.

Step 3: Using textured or embossed fabric in combination with other found objects or small blocks of wood is also worth exploring. While the clay is still flexible, select a couple of sections and manipulate or twist them to distort and stretch the pattern.

Make sure the surface is levelled out again so the top surface will print efficiently. Carefully cut the rest of the panels into smaller, manageable blocks without distorting the impressions, and select the most successful sections. The size of the pieces can vary, and they can be cut to any shape. If a larger panel is required – 3–4in (8–10cm), for example – it may be helpful to bend it into a slight curve, which will help to achieve an even pressure when printing. Remember this will need to be done while the clay is still flexible. If the temptation is to make bigger panels, go ahead, but these will function more like a press mould.

The fragments have been pressed into the soft clay, at different angles, overlapping the images or creating a repetitive pattern.

To produce a cushion-like appearance, the objects are pressed into the clay through a barrier of fine cotton or muslin.

While the clay is still soft, some of the sections can be stretched to distort the image, then twisted into a curve so the design will print evenly.

The edited panels are left to go leather hard, so sections can be cut out of the back of the stamp to create a handle.

The stamps have been fired, so it is time to explore their potential and see what sort of patterned surfaces they can produce.

Testing out the biscuit-fired stamps in soft clay results in a variety of impressions and embossed textures.

Step 4: As the clay blocks will still be quite thick, the next step is to cut out two sections at the back of the stamp to form a handle, making it more user friendly.

Step 5: Once the blocks are completely dry they can be biscuit fired to 1000°C (1800°F), when they will still be porous enough to print successfully.

Step 6: What is quite satisfying about this method is that it is often the rather unassuming fragment that turns out to be a winner and produces a wonderful impression.

Embossed planters by Sarah Pike, using her hand-made engraved stamps to create meticulous designs over the whole surface.

INCISED STAMPS

Incising is the process of engraving lines to create a drawing on the clay surface. When this technique is used to make biscuit stamps, it produces an embossed image when pressed into clay. This type of stamp is very effective for creating dynamic patterns. One simple stamp used repeatedly over a smooth clay surface can transform it into a seemingly complex design.

In theory, incising can be carried out at various stages – when the clay is soft, leather hard, or bone dry, and this will influence the quality of line achieved. Simple graphic designs work well with this technique. It is advisable to engrave the stamps at the leather-hard stage and use a smooth modelling clay as it will produce crisp, clean lines.

Porcelain tends to dry out too quickly and can crack, so it is not suitable for this method. The clay is prepared in the same way as the biscuit stamps, in a thick slab, but make sure the top surface is completely smooth. The clay can be cut into specific shapes at this stage.

Images by the author, taken from her working drawings, then translated into workable designs for the engraved stamps.

Designs can be drawn on to tracing paper and then transferred on to the damp clay using a water-soluble pencil.

Engraving designs into stamps made from different clay bodies, including a more sculptural clay, can yield quite different results.

I will often work out the patterns for this type of stamp using images from my sketchbooks, and will draw them again to simplify the designs, editing sections, making them suitable to be used on a small scale. Designs can be developed from working drawings and sketchbook ideas. Take fragments or sections that can be simplified and that will work on a small scale.

The designs can be transferred, freehand, on to the blocks, lightly drawing with a pencil as a guide. Another option is to transfer the image on to tracing paper using a watercolour pencil, so when the drawn image is pressed on to the surface of the stamp, it will stick to the damp clay and transfer the image.

Let the prepared blocks harden enough so the clay is in the perfect condition to engrave a design. If tackling a collection, it may be wise to wrap the majority in plastic, so they stay in the right consistency while you work on each piece.

Experiment with different incising tools to see which works best for you. It may take a little practice, finding the right angle to use with a tool to get a clean line. A dragging motion will churn up the surface and create too many burrs. To help prevent

Discovering the contrast of printing on clay using a smooth clay stamp as opposed to one made of a sculptural clay body.

Incising the designs into smooth clay with sgraffito tools can become quite additive, and they have such potential when used in different combinations.

fostered this creativity through enrolling her in art classes, and even when she was a small child, inviting her into their own processes, showing her patiently how to hold the tool, how to make that mark, how to build that thing. They gave her the courage to explore new media and ideas on whatever path she chose to follow. She reminisces about the earliest memory of discovering clay: 'It smelled like dirt, like the garden where my mother dug and grew the most beautiful things, like the air after a rain. I remember the sensation of squishing and forming that clay between my little fingers. The magic! Little did I know I'd still be squishing clay through my fingers all these years later!'

Sarah goes on to explain her process:

I carve my 'texture tools', and when I return to the studio, I push them into soft, earthy clay. As I push down, the

this, run the tool at a low angle into the clay, moving the block round, following the direction of the incisions. In the end it is a matter of practice and developing a personal way of working.

During the engraving process, tap the top surface firmly on to the workshop bench, or on a smooth surface that compresses the design slightly, helping to sharpen the image. This can be done a couple of times if needed. As the stamp starts to dry, make any last adjustments using finer tools. At this stage it is worth engraving a mark or arrow on the back of the stamp to use as a reference to guide the position when printing.

Making these stamps can get quite addictive, as the incising method is a very therapeutic process. They have a tactile quality on this scale and resemble decorative building blocks. However, the outcome will be very different if a grittier clay is used, resulting in a more textured, weathered effect.

I have a favourite stamp that I made with a sculptural clay body, so it's worth making some in this type of clay to see the contrast and if they could work well together. Once the stamps have been fired, the designs can be revealed, which is the fun part. Repetitive patterns can be explored, and try out different combinations, grouping the stamps to create more complex designs.

The embossed surfaces that Sarah Pike creates on her ceramics allows the glazes to accentuate the detail.

Sarah Pike: Decorating with Incised Stamps

Sarah Pike has embraced the full potential of decorating with incised stamps and has created a large collection that adorns her work. She is a full-time potter, living and working in Fernie, British Columbia, Canada. She makes functional slab-built pottery in her home studio on an acre of land on the edge of a little ski town.

Sarah grew up in a home of makers. It was normal in her home to make, create and have projects on the go. Her parents

Sarah Pike explores the potential of her stamps by creating repetitive and intricate embossed patterns once the stamps have been biscuit fired.

clay squeezes up into the carved areas of my stamp and creates a raised pattern on the slab's surface. I like to explore shapes that tesselate. I design the stamps so their outside shapes will repeat and fit into each other in different ways. The ogee curve is my most recent obsession. A carved line in the stamp of a specific depth and width will cause the glaze to break over the raised pattern, further accentuating the texture. The glaze surface is soft to the touch. The pattern's texture is like a map for the eyes and fingers to explore.

PLASTER STAMPS

Casting plaster shapes is another way to create linear, embossed designs. Incising into plaster can be a pleasing process and it has a different quality to the surface. Plaster has exceptional properties. It is a hard, absorbent material with a smooth finish, and is the major model-making material in the ceramic world, perfect for achieving fine detail and ideal for making stamps.

As the plaster is much harder, different tools may be needed to engrave the surface. It can be just as addictive and has the advantage of being able to achieve some very fine detailing – even the most subtle of marks and scratches will translate well on to the clay.

To create the shapes for casting, use thick strips of clay about 1in (2.54cm) wide, which can be rolled out and allowed to stiffen a little. I usually start by drawing the outlines of the shapes I want to cast on separate pieces of paper to use as a guide, then arrange the clay strips, echoing the outlines of each drawn shape, creating a continuous upright wall.

A wooden modelling tool or fingertips are used to weld the clay walls to the surface of a thick glass panel or a melamine board on the outside edge, to prevent any plaster from seeping out during the casting process. If the clay is still quite soft either

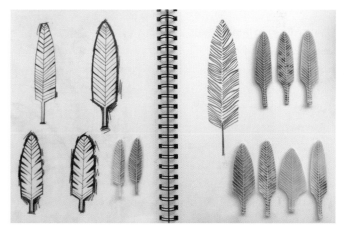

The author's sketchbook ideas for leaf and feather designs for plaster stamps, with some of the test samples in porcelain.

A range of stamp samples by the author, printed on to porcelain and left white to highlight the embossed detail.

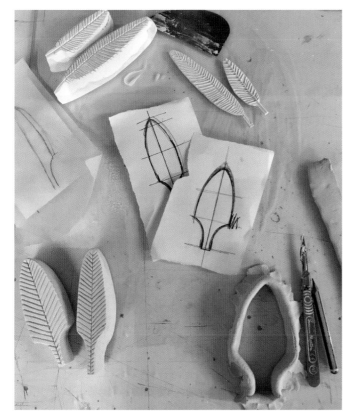

Setting up a stamp mould, ready for casting with clay walls, using the drawn outlines as a guide to constructing the shapes.

These larger versions of a plaster stamp are exploring feather designs, which are transferred to the plaster using tracing paper.

Engraving the design into the plaster with sgraffito and lino tools and using a soft brush to keep the design clear.

leave it to go leather hard, or you can speed up the process with a hairdryer. Be careful not to dry out the walls completely. Although they are relatively small, if the clay walls are still very soft, or too dry for that matter, they risk collapsing when they come in contact with the wet plaster. (Details of how to mix plaster can be found in Chapter 5.)

Let the plaster set and cure completely: take care not to lift the shapes off the casting surface too early as it may result in damaging the lovely smooth surface. The outside shape can be refined with a surform blade or knife before engraving the design into the smooth surface created by the glass panel. This can be done freehand, or drawn in pencil, or use the water-soluble pencil transfer method as described before.

As the image is engraved it can be tested out on a pad of soft clay to monitor the progress of the design and to adjust any marks. It is advisable to start carving as soon as the plaster has set as it will be easier to work with. Carving when the plaster is fully dried will be harder, so it may be helpful to soak the pieces in water. Do make sure that all the plaster components are completely dry before they are used, to ensure they function well.

The clay shapes are fixed on to a smooth surface and a cottle of acrylic tubing is placed round the forms, ready to cast.

SPRIG MOULDS

Another version of creating a decorative surface using plaster resembles a sprig mould, and is carved in the same way as the stamps. Sprigging is a small, decorative element made by pressing soft clay into a small, shallow mould that can be applied to a clay surface to create low relief decoration. Sprig moulds can be made from individually modelled clay forms or found fragments. The design in the mould can be just a simple line engraving, but there is the opportunity to experiment with a more detailed carved pattern.

Sprig moulds and plaster stamps that have been engraved and carved using leaf and feather motifs as inspiration.

Once the plaster is set and the clay former has been removed, the design can be carved in the hollow form.

A positive shape is created in clay, modelling a rounded or angular shape with a flat back, and this is fixed on to a panel of glass or a smooth surface. Wetting the underside should be enough to weld it firmly into place. A strip of clay or a section of acrylic tubing can be used as a cottle. Place it around the clay shape to create the outer wall of the mould, leaving a gap round the form so it resembles a mini press mould. If using acrylic tubing, it is important to saw through the section, to ensure it is flexible enough to be removed easily. It can be secured with sections of tape to the base, but it is advisable also to seal it with clay. The clay form is removed from the centre of the mould after the plaster has set, revealing the negative shape, and after wiping it over with a damp sponge to remove any clay residue, it can be carved with a linear design.

To fill the mould with clay, a small panel of clay is pressed into the hollow form, and rather than wait for the piece to dry enough to drop out, it can be removed by pressing a generous button of clay on to the back of the sprig so it sticks; then with a few tugs, it can be released from the mould. Taking it out of the mould straightaway means the sprig will still be soft enough to work with, and a collection of sprigs can be produced quite quickly from the same mould. If it is quite a shallow form, it can be filled with clay, level to the top of the sprig mould to produce a solid form. The mould will get damp with use, so it may be helpful to dust it with talc to aid removal.

These three-dimensional fragments can be applied to a ceramic surface, or used individually as jewellery components. Make sure when applying a hollow form to another surface that there is a small hole in a discreet place to exclude the possibility of air pockets.

When joining pieces together, score and slurry both surfaces, and press firmly together, being careful not to damage any detail. Be careful not to swamp it with slurry mixture, especially if it is a very delicate sprig, though make sure there is enough to achieve a good bond. Use a wet, soft brush or a very soft finishing sponge to tidy the joins.

Using found objects to create a sprig mould can be very effective, especially if a flexible surface is used, which aids the casting process. Small commercial moulds for making Wagashi, Japanese confectionary, work well. Traditionally made in wood, known as Kashigata, there are flexible versions available made of silicon. The added advantage of these little individual moulds is that they can be filled with plaster to create a positive form to use as a stamp and while the silicon mould is filled with plaster the outside shape can also be cast, creating a sprig mould. The silicon layer separates the two sections, so they can be taken apart very easily by peeling the flexible mould away from the plaster.

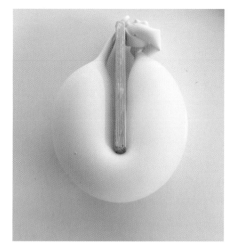

Small modelling balloons are perfect for casting rounded forms, as they are easy to remove and will produce a beautifully smooth surface.

A flexible material that will cast well is silicon, and small catering moulds are ideal to create components, sprig moulds or stamps.

Small moulds made from casting sections of inflated balloons, with acrylic tubing and flexible rubber bowls used as cottles.

A collection of very neat mini moulds, perfect to be used as smooth sprig moulds, or a detailed design can be carved into the surface.

Another flexible material to use when making sprig moulds is an inflated balloon, and using modelling balloons – also known as pencil or twisting balloons – is ideal for working on a smaller scale. They can be manipulated when inflated, tied into sections and curved into shapes.

The most effective way to make a mould when casting this sort of shape is to add the shape to the plaster. A section of acrylic tubing can be used, or a small flexible rubber bowl for mixing plaster is ideal. The liquid plaster is poured in first and then the model is placed in position, so half of the balloon shape is submerged into the wet plaster. If the plaster is allowed to thicken a little, the balloon will stay in position. The form can also be secured with tape or a weight so it will stay level. Be aware that the liquid plaster will rise as the shape is embedded into the mix, so allow for this when pouring the plaster. If the liquid has risen a bit higher than planned, the top can be levelled off with a surform after the balloon has been removed.

CONSTRUCTED STAMPS

I love making this type of stamp as I view them as small sculptural structures and enjoy them as individual objects. I have always found mixed media a tantalizing and often welcome distraction. I usually make the base of these constructions out of wine corks or small blocks of wood.

I tend to build up a collection, so once I have found some interesting fragments, I can put them together. Use a weatherproof wood adhesive or an epoxy resin – what you choose will depend on the sort of materials that are being stuck together. After they have been glued into place, use tape to secure them into position and then leave them overnight to set completely. The stamps can be a diverse range of oddities and can consist of buttons, shell pieces, plastic fragments, torn embroidered fabric and metal washers.

Linocuts work very well, so I have cut and edited some of my past printing experiments and used them in bite-size pieces.

Carving directly into wine corks can be a simple way to make a stamp, but it is advisable to boil or steam them for about ten minutes, which will stop them from crumbling or cracking during the carving process. They can have a dual purpose: to create an embossed detail, and to print colour on to a leather-hard or biscuit-fired surface.

Making mixed-media stamps can be very satisfying, but the excitement is discovering what patterns are revealed when they are pressed into clay.

A collection of small wooden panels, blocks, dowelling and wine corks, used as a based to make constructed stamps.

An eclectic collection of found fragments has been used to make small, constructed stamps that have a sculptural quality.

Edited pieces of lino printing plates, cut into bite-size pieces and glued on to wooden blocks to make constructed stamps.

INTAGLIO STAMPS

These stamps tend to be lower relief: they resemble a collagraph printing plate, and could be used to create an intaglio print on paper. Leaves can be cut in sections, and plant fibres and seeds can be used. Fabric, wool, threads or textured paper will also work with this technique. The fragments are laminated on to panels of sturdy cardboard with several coats of waterproof wood glue to seal them into place. Additional panels of cardboard can be glued on to the back for more support. To make an impression on clay, place the panel face down and press it into place, using a pony roller or rolling pin to get an even pressure on the stamp.

These collagraph-style stamps are constructed from plant fragments and laminated on to sturdy cardboard with a layer of wood glue.

The collagraph stamps produce quite subtle surfaces and fine detail, which is ideal for inlaying oxides or underglaze colour.

EMBOSSED PANELS

These textured stamps can create a more sculptural effect on the clay surface; a modelling paste, also referred to as a sculpting medium, is used for this technique. It is a high-density acrylic paste that contains marble dust and titanium white, and it is used extensively for decorating frames. It dries opaque and to the hardness of stone; it can be textured when wet, and sanded or carved when dry. I love the sculptural approach to this technique: it is a great opportunity to experiment and create very organic textural surfaces, but also sharp graphic images.

Once the paste has hardened, the surface can be carved and incised to develop another layer to the design. Additional layers can be built up to create a very sculptural, undulating surface. There are many versions of this paste available, and some are more flexible, as they are designed to be applied to cloth or canvas. It is advisable to use the stone-like paste as it will render a more effective print.

Use mountboard, firm cardboard or thin wooden panels as a base on which to apply the paste when creating an embossed surface. Stencils can be used if a more precise, graphic image is required.

The paste is spread using a plastic card or a palette knife, through the stencil and on to the card. The result will depend on how the medium is applied, and this will dictate the textural

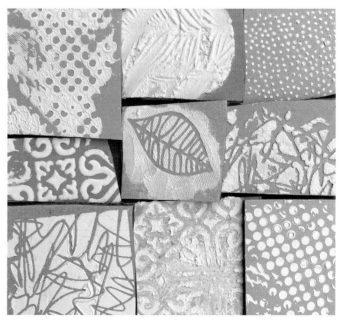

A collection of the completed embossed panels, experimenting with various mixtures of commercial and home-made modelling pastes.

finish. An uneven layering can render interesting results, so it is worth experimenting with the application.

When the panels have dried, they can be glued to a block of wood or additional layers of cardboard to reinforce and support the design, making it more robust for the printing process.

It is also possible to make home-made modelling paste, and a variety of recipes is available. I have experimented with some of the ingredients and have found the most appropriate mixtures to suit this decorative technique. Feel free to adjust the proportions to achieve the right consistency, or add fine sand to the mix for a grittier surface. The paste will keep for months when stored in an airtight jar. I have chosen two recipes as they produce quite different finishes and seem to work quite well.

A thick layer of modelling paste is spread through a stencil, using a knife or a section of plastic card on to a panel of cardboard.

Textured, sculptural marks can be built up in layers, using stencils with the modelling paste, to reveal a detailed embossed surface.

The embossed stamps can prove to be very effective when pressed into soft clay, and create a stone-like surface, depending on the quality of the paste.

Modelling paste recipe 1

| 2 parts toilet tissue |
| 1 part PVA glue |
| 1 part white acrylic paint |

The tissue softens very easily in a small amount of hot water, and the soft mass can be torn up into fragments, before adding the paint and glue. Use a small hand blender to help break up the paper pulp and achieve a workable thick paste. If using this mixture with stencils, leave the stencil in place for a while to allow the mixture to set a little. The embossed pattern will come away from the base if removed too early because of the paper content, which produces a more textural quality.

If the mixture is applied on to a sheet of plastic and allowed to dry for a while, it can be embossed with found objects or biscuit stamps, which can then be removed as a flexible layer. It can be cut into shapes and glued to a panel to use as an embossed stamp, but can also be treated as collage material and pressed into a sketchbook.

Modelling paste recipe 2

1–2 cups baby powder	
½ cup acrylic paint	
¼ cup PVA glue	

These ingredients can be mixed by hand, and a smooth even paste can be achieved very easily; just add more baby powder to thicken the mixture. It works in the same way as the commercial pastes available, and this smoother mixture will produce precise embossed images if stencils are used.

ROULETTES

Rouletting is an ancient technique where an engraved design is applied on to the outside of a cylinder and when rolled over a soft clay slab, will create a continuous embossed pattern. These can be made in several ways and from a variety of different materials.

Clay Roulettes

The roulettes are made using a similar process to clay stamps, using the same sort of clay. Roll out a thinner panel of clay, which can be embossed as before, but curve it into a tube, with the texture facing outwards and while the clay is still flexible. A thick wooden dowel or small cardboard tube is an ideal way to

help control the shape, but twist out the former before joining the edges together with slurry, as it is likely to get stuck if left in place, and could split open as the clay shrinks.

Another option is to use a solid tube of clay, which can be extruded or rolled by hand, with different dimensions and cut into sections. A slim version can be used like a mini rolling pin, but just slightly round the ends so they don't chip.

To apply the detail, roll the clay tube over a textured surface to pick up an embossed design while still soft, or engrave a design when the clay is leather hard. It can be refined with a wet brush for a sharper, more graphic quality, or there is an option at this stage to soften the carving with a smooth damp sponge to produce a more rounded effect. After biscuit firing,

Slim ceramic roulettes and spheres, which are incised with detail or embossed with texture, have been biscuit fired and are ready to decorate a surface.

A collection of roulettes made from clay and plaster, improvising with found materials and upcycling handles from old tools.

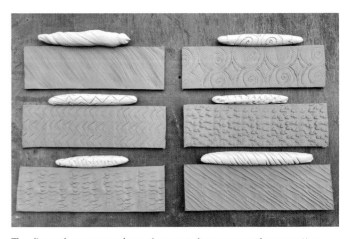

The slim roulettes are an alternative way to impress a continuous pattern over the surface of the clay, and prove to be very effective.

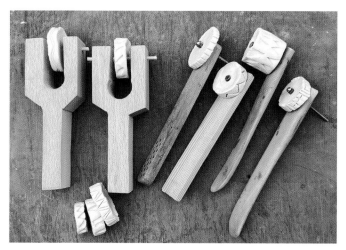

A collection of ceramic wheel-style roulettes, fitted with handles adapted from offcuts of wood and old modelling tools.

Ceramic spheres made in different sizes that have been carved and embossed, designed to create meandering patterns by rolling them over soft clay.

they can be rolled over the clay surface using the fingertips.

If using a thicker section of clay, it may be helpful to fit a handle post firing, so pierce a deep hole at either end or down through the centre using a wooden skewer. The roulettes can also resemble a wheel, which will create a narrow band of decoration. This can be used for repeat patterns, or in combination with other roulettes.

Clay Spheres

A variation on the roulette method that creates a continuous pattern is a biscuit-fired clay sphere. They can be made in different sizes and rolled over soft clay in different directions. The texture can be created by rolling a ball of soft clay carefully over a texture to achieve an embossed design, taking care to keep the shape. Alternatively, carve a simple design that twists over the form once the clay is leather hard. Rolling the fired clay spheres over soft clay in a meandering pattern can undulate and emboss the surface at the same time.

Plaster Roulettes

Using plaster to make roulettes produces a surface on which finer, crisper detail can be incised. Experiment with different tools to explore a more refined approach to carving. The shapes can be cast using small cardboard tubes, making sure they are sealed at the base with soft clay. If an embossed panel of clay is folded round so the texture appears on the inside of the clay tube this can be cast as an alternative to carving. To create a hole down the centre of the roulette, insert a plastic or paper straw in the middle of the mould before casting, secured by a

Rolling the fired clay spheres over the soft clay in a meandering pattern will imprint the surface as pressure is applied.

Small branches have been collected from a walk in the woods, choosing the right proportions to create catapult-style handles for the roulettes.

Small holes have been drilled into the ends of the branches, and the roulettes have been threaded into place with a length of wire.

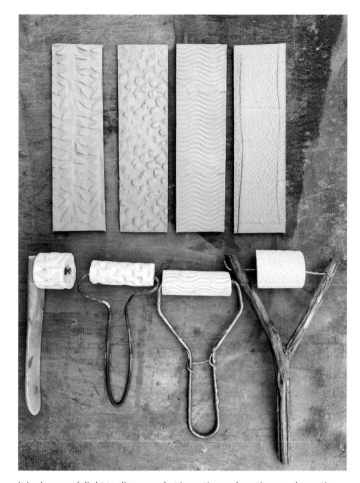

It is always a delight to discover what inventive and continuous decorative patterns the roulettes will reveal.

panel of clay at the base and tape at the top to keep it central. Paint a solution of washing-up liquid with a dash of water over any cardboard or plastic as an extra precaution, and it will aid removal once the plaster has set.

Handles can be fitted on any of the roulettes and can be made of wire or offcuts of wood, and a ready-made handle can even be adapted from old tools. Forage for small branches in a local wood or park to find the right proportions to create catapult-style handles for the roulettes.

PADDLES

Smooth wooden paddles are often used as a forming tool when hand building vessels. Their function is to compress coils or adjust the shape of a form. It is a simple but effective tool, historically one of the earliest and most widely used in Japan,

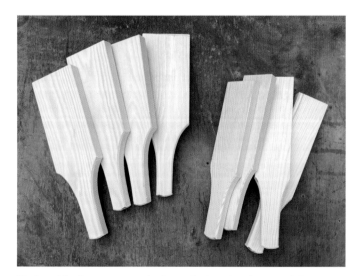

Blank paddle shapes cut out of soft wood using a bandsaw, ready for texture to be applied or glued to the surface.

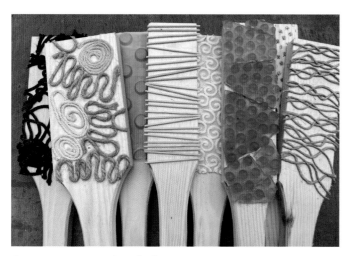

This ancient pottery tool is still a favourite among contemporary makers – these have been adorned with a variety of textures.

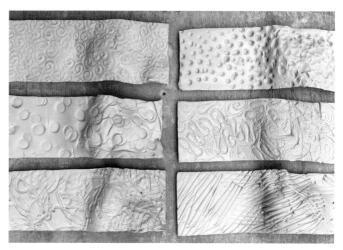

The appeal of the paddle is the different quality of marks it can produce; also the results can be more spontaneous, irregular and erratic.

where it is known as 'Tataki'. It is often used in conjunction with a rounded pebble known as an 'anvil', held against the inside of the vessel as support.

Using a textured paddle can involve changing the shape of the form, creating a more undulating surface and producing an embossed texture all at the same time. By repeatedly applying the paddle, an all-over pattern of overlapping areas of texture can be achieved across the surface. To make paddles, use offcuts of wood as they are bound to vary in proportions and can happily influence how the texture is applied. The profile can be adapted if a handle needs to be cut out with a jigsaw if it is proving too wide to handle comfortably.

The surface of the paddle can have lines engraved into it with a handsaw, distressed with a wire brush or textured with a hammer. More intricate designs can be achieved with wood-carving tools or a high-speed rotary tool. Using hardwood is likely to be more durable but will also produce a distinct impression due to the weight of the wood. Softwood, however, can be used to glue textile pieces, rope and any other collage fragments to the surface with waterproof wood glue. There is the option to add a layer of wood glue over the whole panel, which will not only also seal the surface, but will help to harden the fabric, or leave the textile pieces so they are more porous. Take advantage of the paddles having two sides to create extra patterns.

GLUE DOODLES

This technique can produce very fine linear detail and bold impressions into soft clay. The trailed designs are generated by a using a hot glue pen, trailing, meandering and swirling images on to waxed paper.

The glue will not stick to the surface of the paper and can be peeled away when cool. The pen-style glue gun is ideal for this method as it has more control, and can be precise and quite measured in terms of the glue output. It can make intricate designs and replicates the process of doodling on to paper. The glue doodles can be pressed into the clay individually, using a

A selection of doodle-style designs that can be pressed into clay has been created on waxed paper using a hot glue pen.

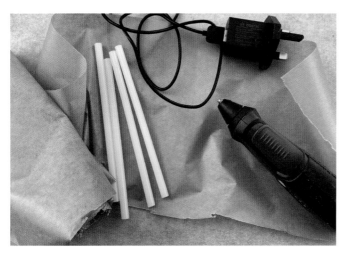

The essential kit for creating glue doodles is a hot glue pen and waxed paper, which prevents the glue from sticking to a surface.

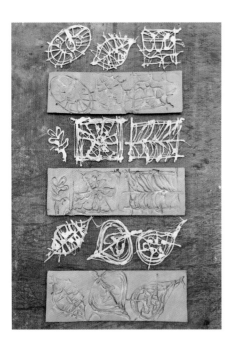

The fine strands of the glue will imprint perfectly into soft clay, and the impressions produced are quite unique.

roller and a sheet of newsprint, or they can also be mounted on to panels of thick card, which can be cut into a shape, reflecting the design; this will leave an outline of the edge of the card when embossed.

ROPE MARKING

Cordage and rope have been used to decorate pottery for many thousands of years, Jomon pots in Japan being some of the earliest examples, dating from around 8000BC.

William Plumptre, Expert in Rope Marking

The ancient technique of rope marking is practised expertly by potter William Plumptre, who trained with Tatsuzo Shimaoka, a Japanese Master Mingei potter. He has been creating works in the anglo-oriental tradition for over three decades. He throws and hand builds classical forms, with a strong commitment to the century-old traditions and skills of the Japanese potters he encountered during his training.

Plumptre first discovered the Zogan technique, which means 'inlay', while working in Mashiko, Japan. This used rope to decorate and indent the surface of the clay, and this printed detail was then filled with painted layers of slip, covering the whole surface; when the surface was almost dry, it was then scraped away to reveal the pattern underneath.

On his return from Japan, Plumptre established a workshop in the Lake District and set about finding a rope maker who was able to make cotton ropes. In Kendal, in Cumbria, there was a long-established rope maker, and William approached him with the idea of using rope to decorate his pots. After some experimentation they made some cotton lays, and he practised using them on clay. It took him a while to be able to use the rope fluently and without leaving an irregular pattern, but in time and with the right stoneware body he was able to produce a reasonable finish.

William says of his research:

What I really wanted was to make my own ropes and patterns, so I started to look at knots and my search took me to Ipswich and a master knot maker of great experience. He taught me in an afternoon the rudiments of Turk head knots and how to weave them. I then spent many months during the winter with dowel and cotton string, weaving a variety of Turk head knots that I could use on my pots; with different thicknesses of cotton I could make larger and smaller knots. The results were intricate finishes on the clay surfaces, which I could inlay with slip. The process of rope decoration is one of endless possibilities, and I never grow tired of the process of roping pots – the rhythmic rolling of the rope on the surface is therapeutic, and the clay lends itself so well to this form of decoration.

William Plumptre's elegant forms illustrate how he has mastered the demanding technique of rope marking. (PHOTO: TONY WEST)

Carefully considered work by potter William Plumptre, who has worked in the anglo-oriental tradition for over three decades. (PHOTO: TONY WEST)

A collection of intricate and skilfully made rope-marking tools by potter William Plumptre, who uses them to emboss the surface of his thrown vessels. (PHOTO: TIREE DAWSON)

CHAPTER 4

SLIP TECHNIQUES

Colour is integral to the allure of working in clay. The delight of exploring the natural palette of different clays and their textural qualities is what is so attractive about the medium. There is also a wealth of ceramic pigments in various forms that can be introduced on to the clay surface or into the body itself. Several of the decorative techniques will use ceramic pigments in some form or another. The most efficient and adaptable way to use colour is in the form of a slip.

Slip is a suspension of clay particles in water, and a simple decorating slip can just consist of the clay that a potter has chosen to work with. Slip has been used to decorate ceramic vessels for centuries, and historically it has been used in so many ways. When a slip is blended with different amounts of oxides or commercial stains it can produce a variety of colours, varying in intensity and tone. The quality of leather-hard clay with freshly applied slip has such great appeal. Adding coloured slip at an early stage can offer more options to build a depth of surface by layering the decorative techniques, first on the wet clay, then at the leather-hard stage.

Slip usually resembles heavy cream and can be applied to soft clay or clay at the leather-hard stage. This means the clay is quite firm but still damp enough to respond well to an application of slip, or several layers. The consistency of the slip can be adjusted to suit the quality of the marks: it can range from a watery type of solution that can allow a darker clay body to show through, to a thick buttery consistency that can be applied with a palette knife or with the fingers. It may be helpful to have a very thick slip and a thinner one to accommodate different methods and applications.

◀ One of the most direct methods for painting detail is using a fine brush, and Jane Muende's work reflects that approach with precision. (PHOTO: MARTA FERNÁNDEZ)

WHAT YOU WILL NEED

When mixing slips or glazes, a sieve will prove to be an essential piece of studio equipment. Plastic containers can be recycled from food storage as they often have efficient lids, ideal for storing slips.

Equipment
- Buckets and containers
- 80-mesh sieve
- Wooden battens
- Stiff washing-up brush
- Firm plastic rib
- Plastic-lidded containers
- Hand blender
- Rolling pin
- Rolling-out cloth or board
- Digital scales
- Measuring jug
- Tablespoon and teaspoon
- Permanent marker
- Hammer
- Commercial brushes
- Heat gun or hairdryer
- Long-nose pliers
- Wooden spatula
- Sgraffito tools

Materials
- Collection of found objects, man-made and natural
- Prepared clay slabs – white body and a dark clay – soft and leather hard
- Dry white clay body or ingredients for a slip
- Oxides and ceramic stains
- Wooden dowels or shaker pegs
- Small branches
- Dried grasses or pine needles
- Rice straw
- Vetiver root
- Cable ties
- String/wool/sturdy thread/raffia
- Dental floss
- Wire

Keep slips in airtight containers to prevent them from drying out; it may help to spray or stir in a little more water occasionally. Avoid applying the thicker type of slip on to very dry clay as it can flake off or cause cracks.

VITREOUS SLIP

Also known as an engobe, or referred to as a fritted slip, a vitreous slip could be described as a cross between a slip and a glaze. Most of the recipes contain a small amount of flux that melts during the firing, acting to bind the slip to the clay surface, making it more versatile: it can be applied to a leather-hard, bone dry and a biscuit-fired surface. It has a self-glazing quality, but can be used in the same way as a regular slip, and can be used on its own as a finished surface. The recipes tend to produce a semi-matt, sheen-like quality when fired to a higher temperature. They can also be used over previously fired glazes, and re-fired to create a varied or weathered surface.

Vitreous slip recipe

China clay	50
Ball clay	33
Potash feldspar	17

Crackle slip recipe

| China clay | 80 |
| Potash feldspar | 20 |

This slip does not create a uniformed crackle surface, but when applied more thickly, fine stress fractures will appear in the surface. An example can be found in on page 172.

MAKING SLIP

The simplest slip recipe is just to use a white clay body. Using the same clay for the slip as is used for making will ensure its compatibility, with fewer risks during the drying and firing process. To mix a slip, make sure the clay is completely dry and broken up into small, manageable pieces. Avoid crushing it too fine and generating too many dust particles – it is advisable to wear a mask during this process.

The essential equipment for mixing a slip: a sieve is an efficient way to eradicate any lumps and achieve an even and smooth mixture.

A more efficient way to reduce the amount of dust is to place the dry clay into a sturdy plastic bag and break it up with a hammer, or use a heavy-duty rolling pin over the fragments. Put a modest amount of hot water in a sturdy container, about a third of the amount of clay to be used: add the dry fragments to the water, and then leave to stand so the clay can slake down evenly. Adding dry ingredients in this way is much safer as it generates far less dust, and a little more water can always be added to ensure the clay is covered completely.

Depending on the amount of clay being used, check the consistency after about an hour. Dry clay will dissolve far more efficiently and quickly than damp, hard clay, which tends to stay lumpy. When it has dissolved and settled, pour off any excess water to create quite a thick mixture. More water can always be added later to adjust the consistency, which is much easier and quicker to do than trying to adapt a slip that is too thin. If this should happen, it can be left overnight to settle again, and then any excess water can be syphoned off. Using a hand blender for smaller batches is a very effective way to mix the slip evenly, and a paddle attachment for a drill can be used for larger amounts. Leaving the mixture to soak overnight will also aid the mixing process and make it easier to sieve.

Set up an 80-mesh sieve over a bucket or large bowl, being mindful to use the appropriate size of the container to accommodate the amount of slip being mixed. Use two batons of wood across the top of the container, so the sieve can rest securely when the slip is poured through. Use a stiff washing-up brush in circular movements to push the liquid through the sieve and eradicate any lumps. A firm plastic rib can also be used for this process but it tends to take a bit longer.

An all-purpose slip is an ideal option if working with different clays at different temperatures. Ball clay tends to feature in most recipes as it is an important ingredient and will fit most clay bodies, and can be easily coloured and fired at different temperatures. The process for mixing the slip from a recipe stays the same as for the clay body slip, adding the dry ingredients to the water rather than the other way around. Making a slip follows the same procedure whatever recipe you decide to use.

Developing a good workshop practice is an important part of this process, making sure that all the ingredients and equipment are ready before you start. Keeping notes throughout the process is vital. Always label newly mixed slips and glazes with a permanent marker on the side of the container or on the lid, as labels don't always stay on.

A task that should become standard procedure when working from a recipe is to keep track by taking notes as each ingredient is measured out.

All-purpose slip recipe

Ball clay	75
China clay	10
Flint	10
Potash feldspar	5

STAINS AND OXIDES

Prepared ceramic pigments, usually referred to as ceramic stains, can expand the potter's creative palette and offer a tantalizing range of possibilities. There are a great many commercial stains now available, alongside metallic oxides, which can be added to a basic white slip to create an expansive range of colours. These pigments can achieve muted tones, subtle pastel shades, or richer, more vibrant slips. It is a matter of experimenting with different amounts of ceramic pigments, individually or in combination to achieve the intensity of colour required. Stains produce a more predictable, repeatable colour, which can be enhanced if used in combination with a transparent glaze. Metallic oxides are more variable and will change colour through the firing process, and will react with different glazes, creating more earthy tones.

All these pigments are concentrated colour, so testing is crucial to finding the right colour, and it is advisable to mix small quantities of coloured slip first to allow for adjustments if needed, before choosing to make a more generous batch.

Ideally colour should be added at the dry stage, which does make it easier to work out an accurate percentage. As a starting point, use 2–10 per cent pigment, especially for the darker stains and oxides, because if they are in stronger saturations, they can cause the surface to bubble and bloat. It is possible to use the lighter ceramic stains in larger quantities, up to 20 per cent to achieve an intense colour.

Most recipes will add up to 100 per cent, which does not include the addition of colour. If you are using 100g of powdered clay or the dry ingredients from a recipe, then add the percentage of pigment also in grams. Feel free to explore the possibilities, using less or more pigments, and even several pigments mixed together in the same batch. Keep a record as you go: it is crucial that you document all your experiments, and label them all clearly. Just keep in mind that the weighing method you employ – grams or ounces, for example – stays consistent throughout all your experiments: it is so important to test.

Another option is to mix a larger batch of white slip and then divide it into smaller amounts in liquid form for testing different colours. Use the same method of measuring throughout this process to ensure the results can be repeated. Use the same cup to measure the slip, which is about 250ml, and if the pigment is measured in level teaspoons, use the same size spoon. It is advisable to add a small amount of water to the dry pigment, mixing it into a paste before adding this to the batches of the slip: this will help to get a good even colour, and sieving at this stage will also help to prevent speckles.

COLOUR STICKS

Coloured slip can be used in a different way when it is processed into thick sticks – these resemble artist's chunky oil pastels and can produce a similar textured mark made by a crayon. A thick slip can be dried out on a plaster block, using a square of cotton fabric to aid removal, modelled into shape and then left to dry completely. If a more intense colour is required, extra ceramic pigment can be added to the slip, or use a batch of stained clay, dried out in the same way. These blocks are left raw and not fired, as they work well in several prints and transfer techniques in powder form. The process uses a small domestic sieve or a food grater to apply the coloured dust over a section of damp clay, through a stencil or on to a surface to be transferred as a print. (Full details concerning these techniques are given in Chapter 5.)

Colour sticks made from coloured slip or stained clay, which have been dried out and modelled into chunky blocks to use in a variety of decorative techniques.

UNDERGLAZE COLOUR

As a complement to the coloured slips and ceramic stains, underglaze colours can work very well in combination or on their own. There is a wide range of commercial colours available in liquid form. They are vibrant, fluxed colours that are very versatile, and can be applied at different stages of the making. They provide a semi-matt surface when left unglazed, and have a slight sheen at a higher temperature; the colour intensifies with a transparent glaze. When they are applied to a biscuit-fired surface, I will often choose to re-fire them before glazing, to fix the colour on to the surface, as they tend to resist the glaze when raw.

There is also the opportunity to apply additional colours, as building up too many layers in one go often means they sink into the surface together – an additional firing between layers can help to prevent this. Underglaze colours and oxides are also available in the form of a wax crayon or pencils, which can emulate the quality of a drawn line. Painting underglaze colour on to a ceramic surface with a fine brush is the most direct method, and using simple repetitive marks can be very effective.

Jane Muende and her Use of Underglaze Colour

London-based artist Jane Muende employs the approach of painting underglaze colour on to a ceramic surface with a fine brush and using simple repetitive marks, and she uses a minimal palette to great effect. She explains:

> I became preoccupied by working in monochrome, enjoying pattern and how the lines interplay. I work intensively, focusing on each methodically drawn, repeated mark using underglaze, wax crayon or painting in wax resist. Where I filter colour into my work, these are mixed by me.

Jane works in porcelain paperclay, as she considers it a 'sensitive medium'. The malleable, translucent, yet robust qualities of the combination of clay and paper enable her to construct her forms. Each piece is hand built and carefully sanded after bisque firing to create a smooth, blank surface on which to draw. She has become completely absorbed by the process of making, from rolling the clay eggshell thin, tearing and pushing it to its limits, gauging the right moment when the clay can be assembled, to the final firing. She describes her approach to decoration thus:

> A thread running through my practice is my concern with the surface, aiming to retain simplicity with the line, pattern, texture, and repeated marks like a sewn stitch. I draw and paint on torn paper and attach them to the bisque work to map ideas and help visualize and decide on the finished piece.

Walking gives her the space needed to visualize and plan the marks and patterns on a piece of work, as well as finding inspiration in the everyday landscape: fences, grills, elongated shadows, patterns on a fabric in a window display will catch her

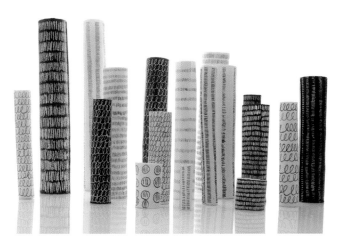

A selection of cylindrical forms by Jane Muende, exploring simple repetitive marks, each methodically drawn. (PHOTO: SYLVAIN DELEU)

When exploring the variation of these simple forms, Jane designs them as a collective and sees the relationship between them as integral to the work. (PHOTO: MARTA FERNÁNDEZ)

eye and appear later in her work. Jane prepares and experiments with an assortment of bottle-neck shapes: tilting, vertical, narrow, wide, each one altering the 'character' of the bottle. The cylinders and bottles are often grouped together in uneven numbers, and they become a 'family'.

MAKING BRUSHES

There has been a long tradition of artists making their own brushes, and potters are no exception. The process is entwined with the ancient slip techniques called Hakeme and Kohiki, developed by the Japanese and Korean potters over centuries, and now popular with potters worldwide. The appeal of making brushes helps to cultivate the qualities that are important and unique to each individual maker. Although manufactured brushes are made to perform well, potters enjoy the challenge of using whatever will work to make the marks they want.

In theory, brushes can be made from any found material, natural or man-made, with an opportunity for them to become quite decorative objects in themselves. They are relatively simple to make so it is worth making a collection and experimenting with a range of different materials. The method of construction is generally the same, regardless of the materials that are used, but there is scope to improvise.

For a free and unlimited supply of organic, natural materials, collect from your garden, the local park, or during those countryside walks. Fresh sections of a plant can be used, but

Jane Muende paints and draws her designs on paper, which she uses as a guide to help plan and visualize the finished piece. (PHOTO: BEN ROSS)

dried fragments will have a stiffness to their structure, making them more suitable to achieving a mark on clay using slips. The softer ones, however, will work better on a biscuit-fired surface, using washes of underglaze or ceramic ink, but also try experimenting with them in a sketchbook using watercolour or coloured inks. They may produce chaotic marks, but they will have a spontaneity and freshness that conventional brushes can't produce.

When collecting very delicate fragments – moss or feathers, for example – these can be tied together with dental floss or fine florist wire on site, so they are ready to put together when back in the studio. They can be bound together in bundles, but

Delicate fragments can be tied in bundles with dental floss or along a length of fine wire, ready to attach to a handle.

Another practical way to integrate the found materials evenly on to the top of a handle is to glue and fold them into a length of cotton fabric.

Brushes made of softer, more fragile materials are ideal for creating painterly, chaotic marks in a sketchbook or on a biscuit-fired surface with ceramic ink.

if they are going to be attached to a handle, twist each fragment separately along a length of the wire: this makes it easier to wrap them round the top of the handle so they are evenly distributed, rather than just tied to one side.

An alternative method can be used if the choice of fragments is proving too tricky to arrange evenly. Place the ends along the middle of a strip of cotton fabric that has been smeared with an all-purpose adhesive or wood glue, and fold it over to hold the ends in place. As the gathered material has a tendency to move around, it can be secured across the middle section to the work surface with some masking tape during the process. The completed panel can be wrapped around the top of a twig, a length of wooden dowelling or recycled paintbrush handle.

Apply a little more glue and bind it tightly with a layer of string over the fabric section to hold it in place and create the ferrule.

Rice straw has traditionally been the material of choice to make Hakeme brushes, and the brush's proportions – it resembles a slender shaving brush – give the potter flexibility of movement and more control to create sweeping and gestural marks. Rice straw is very durable and perfect for slip techniques. It is a by-product of rice production, and is ploughed down in the fields as a soil improver, or used to feed livestock. It is also traditionally used for making domestic brushes: you can therefore purchase a small hearth brush for a modest price and take it apart, and the bristles can then be used to make a range of brushes of different lengths and densities.

Bundles of vetiver, rice straw, pine needles and dry plant fragments are perfect materials to create home-made brushes.

The materials are arranged in a generous cluster and bound together, then string or fabric can be wrapped round the base for a decorative finish.

Another material that has very similar qualities is the vetiver root, an aromatic tall grass native to India. Vetiver is grown for many purposes, such as stabilizing soil, and protecting fields from pests and weeds. It is also used in aromatherapy, cosmetics and herbal remedies. The root system of the vetiver is finely structured and strong, making it ideal to use for making brushes.

Pine needles are another option for trying out the Hakeme method of slip decoration, and can be found in great quantities in late summer and early autumn, scattered under the pine trees as the old needles are shed to allow the new ones to grow. There are often clusters of green needles that have come away after a strong wind, and these can be stripped from the branch if they are still attached. These will eventually start to dry out and lose their colour, but they may also create different marks as they will be a little more flexible.

To make a brush, arrange a cluster of needles, or any other material, so they are all in the same direction and lining up at the base. Hold them together in a bunch with the base of the stems exposed, and bind them tightly together. It can be done initially with wire or cable ties, but do this in at least two places to make it secure, snipping off or flattening any loose ends that are jutting out. The base section can then be wrapped tightly at least halfway, with string or strips of cloth to support the area that will be held in the hand; finish the wrap with a tight knot. The ends can be trimmed to adjust the length of the bristles.

Go one step further and make your own ferrules. A ceramic ferrule can be made in different shapes and proportions, but will need to be a hollow form with an opening at both ends.

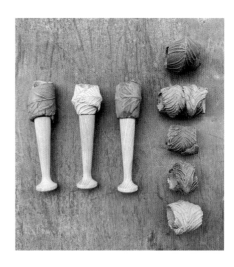

Making ceramic ferrules can add another creative dimension to the home-made brushes; shaker pegs are an ideal solution to use as a handle.

Once they have been fired, a wooden handle can be inserted at one end and glued into place with an epoxy resin. The wood can be sanded or carved should the end need to be adjusted for a perfect fit. Shaker pegs work well as a ready-made handle because they have a tenon joint at the end, which can be slotted into the ferrule very neatly. Just make sure to check the proportions for an accurate fit during the making, and allow for the fact that the clay will shrink.

The cluster of bristles can be bound tightly together with fine florist wire or dental floss, and the base of the bristles is then trimmed to make sure it is level before slotting it into the other end of the ferrule, with a little glue applied into the cavity.

Try out the hand-made brushes on newsprint first, painting with slip, liquid underglazes, oxides or ceramic ink, so you can familiarize yourself with the sort of marks they can produce.

A collection of brushes with hand-made ceramic ferrules. An opportunity to integrate a variety of different handles, including some from vintage tools.

Testing out the more delicate brushes for the first time on paper, to see how they perform using ceramic ink.

Ceramic ink recipe

Calcium borate	30
Potash feldspar	30
Ball clay	25
Flint	15
Bentonite	5
Black stain	10

The dry ingredients are all mixed together before adding water and 5 per cent sodium silicate; then a 100-mesh sieve should be used at least twice to ensure a very smooth mix.

A brush made from a cluster of pine needles: it is more robust, and different movements have revealed different marks.

These gestural painting experiments could be used in some of the transfer techniques when used on paper – further details about this process are featured in Chapter 5. Some medium or CMC gum will need to be added to any oxides, ink or clay slip if these are used for the transfer methods, to make sure they stay on the paper and won't start to flake off as they dry.

Ceramic ink is a perfect option for creating painterly marks, and will also work well on a biscuit-fired surface. Canadian ceramist Robin Hopper, who researched a great deal of ceramic methods and techniques, included a recipe for ceramic ink in his book *Making Marks*.

A stiff brush made from the vetiver root has created scratchier marks; the ink was applied with short, swift movements.

PREPARING SLABS

As a dedicated hand builder, I revel in how ideas develop out of the processes and experiments with materials and techniques. Working with slabs or sheets of clay is an essential part of my working process. There are different ways to approach this: rolling out using a rolling pin, slicing from a block with a bow harp, using a slab roller, or throwing the clay down repeatedly to stretch it out. I have used all these methods, and sometimes combined them. I tend to use a bow harp or wire to slice an even but generous slab, and then a rolling pin. A slab roller comes into its own when slabs need to be produced in large quantities.

I first thump out the clay with a mallet or with my fist to get it to a more manageable thickness to roll out. I favour a vintage lead dressing tool, which is the perfect shape to even the clay out. During the whole process I turn the clay over several times to ensure an even compression on both sides. I use wooden battens as guides to achieve a perfectly flat slab at the right thickness. I then smooth and compress the surface of the slab on both sides with a damp rib. All these different movements help to reduce cracking and warping.

I use a smooth cloth or panels of chipboard to roll out the clay, and have a few extra boards to hand, so I don't have to move the prepared slabs too much and can give them time to stiffen a little. It is important not to over-handle them as they can be distorted and easily stretched. They can be used when they are freshly made as a soft slab, or when partially dry at the leather-hard stage. Soft slabs allow you to curve, manipulate and modify the shape, and hardened slabs become a perfect canvas for an array of decorating techniques.

The ancient technique of Hakeme can stand alone as a decorative method of applying slip, creating a lively and gestural surface.

SLIP APPLICATION

The wetter the clay when the slip is applied, the thinner the coverage will be, and the longer it will take to dry between coats. Slip will not run, move or mix unless you intend it to. The slip decoration will remain the same after firing because it is fused on to the surface and won't come off. It will appear lighter, but the colours will darken when fired to a higher temperature. Slip will allow the flexibility to create exact patterns, unlike glaze, which can blend or blur together during the firing. It can be used freely and layered using a variety of techniques, and any mistakes can be wiped away, scraped back or painted over. Some of the decorative techniques require the clay to be at the leather-hard stage to work well. This means the clay needs to be firm enough to hold its shape so it can absorb the liquid slip efficiently.

The Hakeme Technique

Japanese potters have been practising this lively method of slip decoration for centuries, which translates as 'brush grain'. It originated in Korea and is known as *gye yal*, and it began as a technique to ensure a workmanlike covering of their vessels with slip and to ensure it stayed on the clay surface.

A generous layer of creamy white slip is applied to a dark clay body that is nearly leather hard, using a soft, flat brush.

A home-made brush made from strong vetiver roots is dragged across the slipped surface creating meandering and swirling patterns.

The Japanese described it as 'the rough touch'. It then developed into a decorative feature, and its spontaneous and natural approach enticed the Japanese tea masters to adopt it as their own. Traditionally a white slip is used over a dark body, as the gestural marks created by the rice straw or pine-needle bundles reveal the dark colour of the clay through the slip. The pressure and quality of the brush during the application can determine how textural and linear the marks can be.

The slip should have a thick, creamy consistency. When applying it with a hand-made brush, make sure the brush is coated with a generous amount and then drag it over the surface in swift, spontaneous strokes.

Alternatively, a thick layer of slip can be applied with a softer brush or poured over the clay surface first, and the Hakeme brush can then be dragged through the slipped surface while it is still wet to leave a swirling or striated pattern.

In both cases, this technique demands some practice – it requires an intuitive approach, and is best executed rapidly and with confidence. In traditional Japanese aesthetics, wabi-sabi is a view or thought on finding beauty in the imperfect. This meditative approach is perfect for the transient style this method demands.

When the slip is allowed to dry a little, a sgraffito pattern can be incised quickly through the slip as an additional dimension to the painterly decoration. Once fired, there is also the option to add painted or printed detail with oxides or underglaze colours before glazing. If there is only a light clay body available, a dark iron wash or ochre slip can be applied before the white slip, to create the contrast, allowing the individual slip layers to have time to dry so the shine has gone. Alternatively, a dark slip can be used over the light body, using the same method of application.

Finger Swiping

A decorative effect that is far freer and softer in appearance is made by sweeping the fingers through the wet slip, and the displacement on either side of each stroke can add to the effect as it reveals the clay or colour beneath. A generous coating of slip is applied, and then expressive marks are made, swiftly and directly with the fingertips. As well as drawing through the slip, hands can be used to apply the slip directly to the clay surface. The white slip can vary in tones as a darker clay body or slip is merged into the mixture. This technique can be used at the glazing stage, and works best when the glaze is still wet. Having a contrasting slip colour applied before the biscuit firing will give more emphasis to your design, as the surface will be revealed in the glazing process.

Hilary Mayo and her Use of the Finger-Swiping Technique

Hilary Mayo is a ceramic artist who has incorporated the finger-swiping technique into her repertoire of surface decoration. She specializes in hand-building techniques, with a focus on vessel forms, but her sensitive surfaces are a response to places and experiences, abstracted images of landscape. Her work is informed by the geology and topography of the Icelandic landscape, and most recently of the Suffolk coast, where erosion is a constant theme. The vessels are constructed with finely rolled slabs of stoneware clay, and she subtly manipulates the walls to form a canvas.

Layers of black and white porcelain slip are applied to the surface, and Hilary tries to keep the layers loose and painterly, so each piece is unique.

She uses her fingers to manipulate the slip, creating an abstract landscape. She explains the process thus: 'I have to work very quickly, and there's no going back. Once the slip is applied it has to be left.' Hilary has a large collection of brushes, but this technique creates the movement and spontaneity that she requires, and she finds it is a useful way to add spontaneity to a controlled process.

Once the slip has become leather hard, Hilary can add the final decorative elements before allowing it to dry slowly and take it through a biscuit firing. Using fingers again and a stiff brush to complete the piece, the dark slip is splattered and flicked over selected areas on the white slip.

Hilary has a meticulous process for applying glaze to the fired work: details of her technique can be found in Chapter 8.

Hilary Mayo hand builds her vessel forms and subtly manipulates the walls to form a canvas on which she applies layer upon layer of slip. (PHOTO: CHRISTIAN BARNETT)

Hilary paints over the whole surface with several layers of a rich black slip, using a hake brush to ensure an even coverage. (PHOTO: CHRISTIAN BARNETT)

Layers of white slip are applied over the dark slip at the base of the vessel to reflect a sense of place. (PHOTO: CHRISTIAN BARNETT)

Hilary uses her fingers to move the slip around on the surface – she must work quickly and spontaneously to achieve the right marks. (PHOTO: CHRISTIAN BARNETT)

Final details are added once the slipped layers have lost their shine, using fingers again to flick and splatter with the black slip. (PHOTO: CHRISTIAN BARNETT)

One of the series of Icelandic vessels by Hilary Mayo; she also used her hands to apply some of the detail. (PHOTO: MARY LLOYD DAVIES)

Marlene Gartner has created *Blue Girl, Longing for Austria*. Most of her work features a narrative element, reflecting her surroundings and daily life.

Detail of one of Jessica Merle's 'Lalaloopsy' plates using the sgraffito technique combined with the smoky effects of a saggar firing.

SGRAFFITO

Sgraffito is a form of incising into clay and comes from the Italian 'graffiare' meaning 'to scratch'. This technique can be carried out at different stages, each producing different results, so it is worth exploring all the options. Sgraffito remains a popular method among students as it does not require the same speed and assurance as some of the brush techniques. The simplicity of this approach to making marks enables a direct form of expression, and for a maker can lead to a life-long passion. The procedure is usually done through a layer of slip that is a contrasting colour to the clay body. Cutting into a leather-hard slip will give a clear line, and any residue clay will come away cleanly. Sgraffito can also be done directly into the clay, and this epitomizes the quality of bold drawings on paper.

This type of sgraffito drawing can be enhanced by filling the engraved lines with a wash of oxides or underglaze colour after the biscuit firing. Wiping away the residual pigment will highlight the drawing in the surface. Alternatively, dry colour can be dusted into the line using a ball of cotton wool, wiping away any residual colour with dry fingers and compacting it into the detail – a damp sponge will incline to take the colour straight out again. A dab of glaze over the powdered surface can help to seal the colour. Working with softer clay will produce large burrs as the tool cuts into the clay. It is advisable to leave them in place until the surface has dried enough to prevent damage to the design, and then they can be brushed away. When drawing a design into the surface when the clay is bone dry, the results will vary and may chip, resulting in irregular lines, which can also be effective.

Jessica Merle and her Use of the Sgraffito Technique

Jessica Merle, a ceramist from Durban, South Africa, uses some of these drawing methods in her sgraffito technique, resulting in a very intuitive approach to her work. Her 'Lalaloopsy' series sprang from experiments in translating mixed-media collages

The combined method of glazing and saggar firing adds to the unpredictable nature of the process and enhances the sgraffito detail.

To form the Lalaloopsy plates Jessica roughly rolls out slabs, allowing their shapes to become uneven and their edges to crack, and then drapes them over plaster moulds. Once the plates are leather hard, she paints them with slip and then incises into them – she tends to approach this part of the process by following her creative instinct. She is interested in colour, and applies earthenware glazes in painterly applications.

After the glaze firing, individual saggars are made by laying organic materials such as feathers, eggshells and shed snake skins against the surface of each piece, and wrapping them up in newspaper or aluminium foil. She fires the saggars in a barrel, with the fire reaching around 680°C. The carbon deposits of the saggar firing interact with the glazed and unglazed areas of the ceramic surface. Sometimes a piece becomes completely blackened except for the glazed areas; at other times the carbon accumulates in the cracks of the glaze or sits on the surface as shiny metallic marks. Jessica says:

> Combining glazing and saggar firing develops a depth of surface and sense of layering that speaks of archaeology and the objects found throughout the history of our human material culture. The unpredictable nature of saggar firing is juxtaposed with the controllable qualities of glazing, creating the impression of movement and life in a piece.

More information regarding this approach of creating marks using smoke firing methods with combustibles can be found in Chapter 8.

Experiment and Prepare

There is a wide selection of tools available from ceramic suppliers, designed specifically for incising detail, and some are featured in the tool list in Chapter 2 – but experiment with wooden modelling tools, lino cutting tools and even dentists' tools, as they all have potential. It is a matter of experimenting and finding what works. The type of marks that can be created can comprise deep or shallow marks, linear designs and very intricate illustrations.

The first step with a more illustrative sgraffito technique is to plan the design so decisions can be made about where to carve. Creating a line drawing on paper as a starting point will help to achieve the right balance in the image. To prepare a slab for the sgraffito technique, make sure the clay is just past the leather-hard stage, as it needs to be a little drier than you

on to a ceramic surface, discovering how the ceramic process offered her more opportunity for mark making and creating a depth of surface. The recurring 'loop-de-loop' pattern is inspired by asemic and automatic writing, as she says, 'representing a playful discovery and the winding path of being human'. The title comes from the Lalaloopsy rag dolls, a name that conjures up silliness and imagination. Jessica describes her process:

> I love that asemic writing can 'encode' messages, and I play to this secretive trait by scratching in song lyrics, thoughts in my head, and words I want to say to people. I prefer to use wooden tools for this process, although I usually find myself trying different tools until I find the one that feels right for a particular piece. To further add to the mark making of the work I use brushes that leave bristly scratches in the slip rather than creating a uniform surface.

think. For a strong graphic result use a smooth white body and a strong dark colour – this can also be reversed. Use a black liquid underglaze or a dark clay slip, and there is also no reason why different colours cannot be included.

Marlene Gartner and her Use of the Sgraffito Technique

Ceramic designer Marlene Gartner has started to explore the sgraffito method with great enthusiasm, and has been testing a variety of coloured slips and translating her designs from her sketchbooks. They help her plan what she wants to draw into the clay and to see how it could look. But when she starts to carve it is mostly by intuition, taking the sketches more as an inspiration rather than just copying them.

She paints several even layers of coloured slip over the surface, letting the shine go off between each layer, which may take several even coats to achieve a good dense coverage as the clay is damp. When the surface is touch dry, she starts to apply her design. It is drawn freehand on the clay with a pencil, which will be visible on the surface and will act as a guide.

Marlene starts by engraving just the outline, so she can plan the complete layout of her design across the clay surface. As she engraves the drawing, the burrs and clay fragments are swept away using a soft brush, to help keep the carving clear for a neat result. The next stage is to tackle the background and carve areas away with repetitive strokes.

Thin slivers of colour can be left in the background, but Marlene chooses to engrave the background colour away completely, to create a stronger contrast. Her consideration is a good balance between the sgraffito detail and the colour of the clay body, as this will ensure a stronger impact when the

Marlene Gartner has painted a range of test pieces with different coloured slips on a variety of clays, to explore the sgraffito technique.

All the test fragments are laid out after firing; Marlene has chosen to use a white clay body on some as a contrast to the darker clay.

Using her sketchbook ideas as reference, Marlene engraves a white clay body, using a slip that will fire to a rich dark green.

A collection of Marlene Gartner's larger, sculptural forms drying in the Academy's studio, waiting to be fired and reflecting different aspects of her visual research.

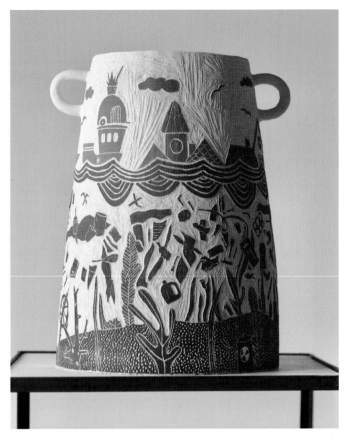

Marlene's most recent work has revealed simpler, bolder structures, but with colourful layers to enhance the sgraffito detail.

clay is glazed. She works with a variety of stoneware clays and applies a very thin layer of glaze to enhance the colour.

Marlene, who is originally from Austria, lives with her family on their 120-year-old boat, *Mauna Trio*, in Denmark. She had been working in film for several years before deciding that she needed a new orientation to her life. Ceramics had been always a big dream, so she applied to the Royal Danish Academy of Design in Copenhagen. The glass and ceramics programme is located on the remote but beautiful island of Bornholm, and is one of Europe's leading educational institutions in this field; it has a strong international element as the programme is in English. While learning and exploring different techniques, Marlene became fascinated by the sgraffito method and wanted to explore further. The carving into leather-hard clay she found extremely satisfying, and it quickly became integrated into her approach of working with ceramics; it is now the main element of her artistic expression.

For the moment she says: 'I am trying to balance "mama-life" and am devoting myself to my craft, which can be quite the challenge, since both sides of my life can absorb me completely.'

Rieko Miyagi and her Use of the Sgraffito Technique

Reiko is a Japanese potter who worked as a professional maker before relocating to the USA and settled in North Carolina. She uses the sgraffito technique as her main method to decorate her work, and prefers to limit the colour to emphasize the contrast of the colour of the clay with her designs. She says: 'By using a carving technique such as sgraffito I can bring depth and texture to the surface. It helps to give not only a bold look, but also an organic feel to the work, which works well for the rustic and primitive motifs that I like to draw.'

Japan is the country where the animistic belief of 'Yaoyorozu no kami' – or literally, 'God in eight million things' – is still alive in life, culture and the arts. Rieko draws a lot of animals, birds and botanical images, often combined with symbols and patterns inspired by traditional folklore or tribal work. She uses the clay as a canvas to tell her 'Yaoyorozu no kami' stories, which she says: '...is the connectedness of all beings and an appreciation of our surroundings, which makes us what we are.'

To prepare the work for carving, Reiko applies two, or three even coats of underglaze colour to the surface, and starts by carving a deep outline of the shapes – though sometimes she will use wax resist to create the outline of the object before applying the underglaze. This method tends to be less controlling and more unpredictable, resulting in a more whimsical and wilder look.

Reiko uses a variety of tools to sgraffito into the leather-hard clay to reveal her intricate designs as the background is carved away.

Reiko Miyagi has chosen the sgraffito technique to create the variety of animal and bird motifs that grace her designs.

Her favourite tool for sgraffito is a xacto craft knife, which is very similar to a scalpel, because it can achieve a variety of line widths. She uses a sharp blade for thin lines and a worn-out blade for the wider lines. She employs a variety of line widths for carving, depending on the look that she wants to achieve; she also uses needle tools, with both a sharp and a dull tip for carving circular lines, and ribbon-style loop tools to carve out larger areas. She explains: 'I want to keep an organic and warm character that offers the beholder of my work a moment of tranquillity or joy in their daily life.'

COMBING

Combing is another direct way of creating fluid marks by dragging different serrated tools across the clay surface. In Japan it is referred to as 'Kushime'. Combing can be done through a slip in the same manner as Hakeme, or directly into a soft clay surface, but it results in more defined marks. Timing is

Reiko uses the clay as a canvas to tell her *Yaoyorozu No Kami* stories, influenced by her Japanese upbringing, its culture and the arts.

Combing effects can be created with a variety of serrated tools of different sizes – exploring their potential is part of the creative journey.

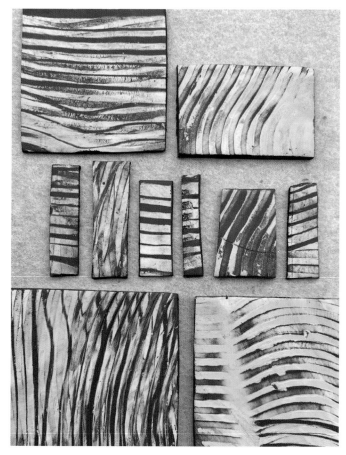

Test samples of the layered slip technique, using a smooth black earthenware clay as the base, which gives a slightly softer effect.

important to comb effectively through slips. Making sure the slip is the right consistency is important: if it is too wet the detail will settle back again, too dry and the ability to produce fluid marks is lost.

The type of tool and the quality of the clay will dictate the combed lines. The tools can be made of metal, wood or plastic. There are pottery tools specially designed for this method, but decorator's tools used for woodgraining, glue or paint effects work well too. Notches can be cut into a plastic card, and even the humble fork comes into its own as a perfect tool to incise. Grog or sand in the body will result in a coarser line and a more broken edge, which can be very effective, and selecting the right type of glaze can emphasize the quality of the marks.

LAYERED SLIP TECHNIQUE

The layered slip technique is similar to the sgraffito and combing methods for making marks, but involves using layers of colour. It starts with a modest, painterly approach of applying different coloured slips or underglazes, but is transformed by engraving through the layers of slip, revealing a rich and intricately patterned surface.

Step 1: A layer of black slip or underglaze is painted over the whole surface of a freshly rolled out panel of clay.

Step 2: Once the shine has gone, several different colours are applied over the black base. It can be painted with gestural marks and the thickness can vary, to generate a painterly surface.

A generous layer of black slip or underglaze is applied evenly over the whole surface of the clay panel and allowed to dry enough to lose its shine.

Several different underglaze colours are painted over the black surface in a painterly and gestural way, playing with the thickness of the colour.

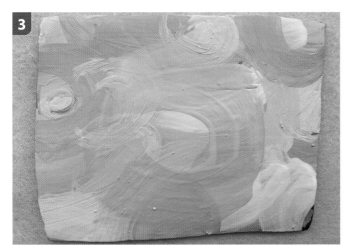

Once the colour has lost its shine, a second layer is applied, making sure the colours are mixed around to contrast with the first layer.

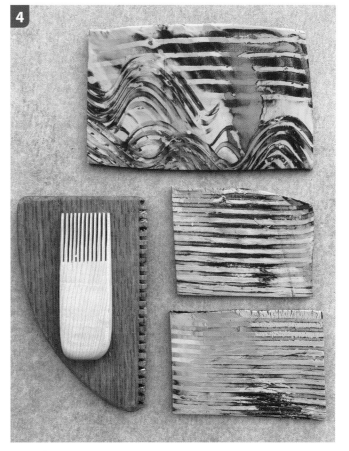

The surface is engraved with a serrated tool, revealing a complex design; the panel is then compressed through newsprint with a rolling pin to stretch the image.

Step 3: Once the surface has lost its shine, another layer of colours is applied and these are moved around to contrast with the first layer.

Step 4: When the layers of colour are no longer tacky, a serrated rib is used to scrape through the surface in different directions to reveal a complex pattern. The panel is placed between sheets of newsprint and rolled out a bit further with a rolling pin, to stretch and compress the image.

THE KOHIKI TECHNIQUE

The Kohiki style of mark making derives from a method adopted by the Korean potters in Japan, and is closely associated with the tea ceremony. Kohiki refers to a dark clay body covered in white slip, but this version involves a process of stretching the clay to cause the slip to crack apart and distort on the surface. This technique can produce a dynamic layer, and transform a smooth white slip into a textured surface, taking on the characteristics of weathered stone, ancient tree bark or a dried riverbed.

There is a specific slip recipe to use with this technique, which enables the slip to dry a lot faster than the clay and assists with the development of distressed creative marks. For the stretching process use an absorbent surface – a wooden workshop bench will work well, or a panel of cement board. If there is a risk of the clay sticking during the procedure, dust the surface lightly with talc.

Two different home-made brushes are used to drag through the wet slip, creating a meandering repetitive mark, exposing some of the dark clay body.

Kohiki slip recipe

China clay	35
Fireclay	30
Nepheline syenite	25
Wollastonite	10

When mixing the Kohiki slip, aim for a thick consistency, and be generous with the layer of slip applied to the clay slab. This can be poured or painted on with a broad, flat brush. Make sure the slab is thick enough to allow it to be stretched, as it will be made thinner by the process. While the slip is still wet, a repetitive pattern is created using a stiff brush, dragging it through the slip, taking some slip away in the process. It can be a brush that has been trimmed to give an uneven mark, or a hand-made Hakeme-style brush will also work well.

The drying process can be speeded up with a heat gun, but keep it moving over the surface, just until the slip loses its shine and is matt in appearance. Lift the slab and flex it in your hands to see if small cracks start to appear in the slip. Throw it down on to the table or a board, not too harshly, in a swift, sweeping, inward motion, just enough to stretch it gradually. Repeat the action, stretching in different directions until a defined distressed pattern starts to appear, which will resemble a rocky surface.

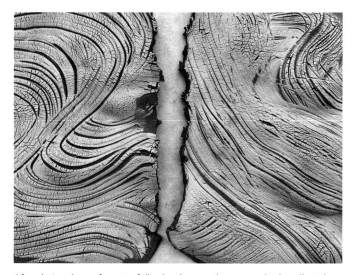

After drying the surface carefully, the clay panels are stretched to allow the slip to crack and distort, revealing a distressed surface.

When handling the textured panel, be careful to avoid damaging the decorative surface, and to prevent any smudges, make sure your hands are kept clean during the process. To undulate the surface a little more and accentuate the cracks in the slip, it can be manipulated by stroking the back of the panel with fingertips.

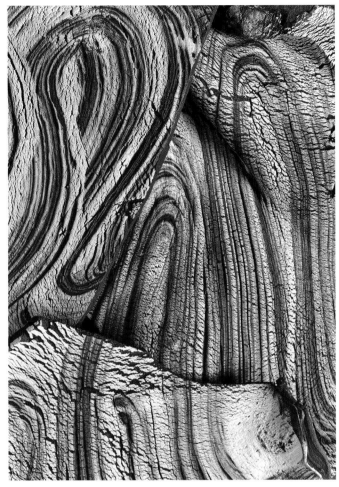

The panels have fired darker and provide a sharp contrast between the slip and clay, highlighting the ripples and the fractured surface.

Hot glue doodles and constructed stamps are ideal for creating suitable impressions to use with the Mishima technique.

MISHIMA

The ancient art of inlaying slips came from the Japanese island of Mishima, but originated in Korea around the sixteenth century; it is known as '*sang gam*'. This involves incising into a smooth, leather-hard clay and filling the details with layers of a contrasting slip. The design is revealed when the excess slip is scraped away and the inlaid design becomes flush with the surface of the clay. The engraving can be composed of fine lines or deeper marks, depending on the design. Stamps can also be used to create impressions into the clay, which can be filled with colour. The most appropriate stamps that will create the right impressions for the Mishima technique are glue doodles, constructed stamps and collagraph-style stamps. A dusting of talc can be used to aid the printing, and this should be done when the clay is soft.

When engraving, the method will generate burrs of clay, and these should be brushed away regularly with a dry, soft brush.

The slip is painted into the design, making sure that the engraved lines are filled completely to the level of the clay surface – this will take several coats, as the layers will sink down into the design as they dry. Coloured clay can be rolled out into thin coils and these impressed into the detail or smeared into the surface; they may need a light misting of water so they don't dry out. The excess colour is scraped away from the surface using a metal rib or a looped tool once the slip or colour has reached the leather-hard stage.

This technique may take a little practice, the aim being to remove just the colour and not too much clay, otherwise the design can be reduced or may even disappear. A very smooth clay is ideal for this method, as any grog present in the body will jeopardize a clean, sharp edge to the inlay.

An alternative method to creating engraved detail, or if a background colour is required, is when the inlay is done using wax and underglaze colour. The base colours can be painted on to a leather-hard surface and allowed to dry enough so that an even layer of water-based wax can be painted over the whole surface and left to dry.

The design can be scratched into the surface, and a soft brush used to clear away the burrs during the process. A darker contrasting underglaze can be painted into the lines, making sure that the cavities are filled completely. A soft, clean sponge is used to clear away any colour left on the surface, using clean water and rinsing the sponge at regular intervals until the design is exposed. A hot glue-pen doodle can be impressed into the surface of the clay before the application of wax: when this is removed, a cavity is revealed that can be filled with colour. The biscuit firing will burn away the wax layer. With both techniques a light sanding with wet-and-dry sandpaper can refine and smooth away any blemishes or smudges left on the surface.

Layers of white slip are scraped away from a leather-hard surface using a metal kidney, to reveal the design inlaid into the clay.

An alternative method to creating inlaid detail is to engrave through a layer of wax, in combination with colour or a glue doodle stamp.

The Mishima technique can produce a wide diversity of inlaid designs using different methods to create the surface.

Fragments of glue doodles have been embedded into the clay to produce a graphic design, then filled with a fine porcelain slip, to create an inlaid surface.

CHAPTER 5

PRINTING AND TRANSFER

Clay and print share a long history, and printmaking is an artistic process that has held a great fascination for me since discovering the delights of this technique during visits to the print room as part of my degree course. What is so versatile about many of the printing methods that are traditionally used on paper, is that they can be adapted to print slip, underglaze colour or oxide on to a clay surface at different stages of the making process.

The principle of transferring images from one surface to another can be so satisfying. I love the fact that I can combine my experience as a maker and merge it with my passion for printmaking. The experimental approach to printmaking has stayed with me, and I have adapted and developed these methods over time, and have incorporated them into a variety of different ceramic projects for students over the years. Some of the direct printing methods require no specialist equipment, and this initial low-tech approach will allow you to explore the techniques and evaluate the different surface qualities that are on offer. There is also the opportunity to translate your ideas using a design software program so they can be transformed into stencils or stamps which can be digitally cut.

WHAT YOU WILL NEED

This list features all the equipment and materials required for a variety of printing techniques, including materials needed to create different types of stencils. Try out the different options, or just select and use the equipment or resources you have available.

- Transparent copier film
- Opaque marker
- Sturdy glass panel
- Wooden cottles
- Flexible plaster mixing bowl/plastic containers
- Mask, when using dry materials
- Scissors
- Brushes

Equipment
- Soldering iron
- Scalpel
- Cutting mat
- Tyvek paper
- Heated stencil cutter
- Polyester stencil sheets
- Digital stencil cutter
- Commercial stencils
- Exposure board kit
- Pre-coated emulsion stencil film

Materials
- Potter's plaster
- Decorating slips
- Liquid underglaze colours
- Silkscreen medium/CMC
- Newsprint
- Smooth cotton cloth/ textured fabric
- Washing-up sponges
- Thin card
- Gaffer tape

MIXING PLASTER

Learning how to mix plaster is such a useful skill to have, with so many occasions to use plaster in decorative techniques, methods of making and constructing moulds. It is such a versatile ingredient for the potter, and has great potential. Plaster is provided in powder form, and when mixed with water has the unique properties of becoming hard and absorbent with a wonderfully smooth surface. It can pick up fine detail, and its porous quality makes it ideal for slip casting and a variety of press moulding techniques, and experimenting with liquid paperclay and slips.

◀ A print made from one of the experimental transfer sheets, using underglaze colour applied with sponge stamps and sweeping brushstrokes.

It is important to prepare the work area and set up all the equipment ready for casting, before starting to mix the plaster.

Each section of the wooden cottle has a block attached at one end, so the clamps can secure the unit at each corner and be adjusted to any size.

It is important to prepare the work area so that everything is set up, ready to start. There are a few guidelines and practical workshop procedures to be considered when mixing any amounts of plaster. Always use cold water, as hot water will speed up the process of the plaster going solid. Make sure no plaster goes down the sink into the drain – even small amounts will accumulate over time and cause problems. Have a bucket fitted with a plastic bag or bin liner, filled with water, for rinsing hands and wiping out any containers. Any plaster in the water can be allowed to settle, pour off the water and discard the bag. If using flexible plaster mixing bowls to mix plaster, any residue can be left to dry and can be easily released just by squeezing the bowl. Other containers – a small bucket or bowl, for example – can be lined with a plastic bag, and the dregs of plaster can be left to harden and the bag thrown away, keeping the containers clean.

COTTLES

A cottle is a wall, constructed to contain the plaster when making a mould. It can be made from different materials, usually dictated by the shape of the model that needs casting. A flexible plastic sheet works well, as it can be cut to size and will release easily from the plaster; it is used for moulds that require a curved wall, and can be secured with gaffer tape and clay. Clay is generally the choice for smaller casting projects such as sprigging and does not require soaping. Plywood boards or melamine-faced timber boards are recommended for larger amounts of plaster. A set of four panels with 2 × 2in blocks (5 × 5cm) fitted at one end, enables them to be adjusted to any size and then clamped into place at each corner to ensure a professional finish to the moulds. As a guide, they can be 6–8in (15–20cm) wide, and around 14–18in (36–46cm) long. For an easy release, the plywood should be treated with soft soap, petroleum jelly or oil soap before each use.

CASTING A PLASTER BLOCK

Plaster blocks have proved to be one of the most useful pieces of equipment I have in the studio, as they can be used for a variety of decorative techniques. I have several in A4 size – 8¼ × 11¾in (21 × 29.7cm) – which are a practical size to use, but I have also cast a few larger ones for more adventurous projects.

I used a thick panel of glass as a base for the blocks as this produces a very smooth, polished surface. In this case the cottles can be made of strips of plywood or leather-hard clay about 4in (10.16cm) wide to create the edge of the mould. Make sure that whatever system is used, they are sealed firmly to the glass, with extra clay applied to all the seams to avoid any plaster seeping out. The block should be at least 2½in (6.35cm) thick when cast; this helps with absorbing the moisture from wet clay or slip and will not get too saturated. There are many kinds of specialist plasters available, but I would recommend potter's plaster, a general all-purpose plaster that is suitable for the methods used in this book.

The process I use for mixing plaster is often referred to as the 'pyramid' or 'island' method. It doesn't involve measuring, but requires you to evaluate the amount of plaster needed. Have some smooth plastic containers or small moulds at the ready to use up any plaster that might be left over.

Fill the container with cold water, allowing enough room for the liquid to swell during the mixing process. Always add the plaster to the water, and be careful not to pile the plaster in too quickly as this will create a lumpy mixture. It is advisable to wear a mask as this stage. Sprinkle generous handfuls of plaster evenly over the whole surface of the water, and keep adding until a mound of plaster is peaking above the water level. Allow it to settle, and once all the plaster has been absorbed, place a hand down to the bottom of the container, massaging away any lumps. Wave your hand in a drifting action under the surface to encourage the air bubbles to come to the top.

Continue this movement, making sure it is a smooth, even mixture, and eventually the plaster will gradually start to thicken. 'Marking' is a way to determine when it is ready. Run a finger in a criss-cross pattern over the surface of the plaster, and when it leaves an impression, it is ready to pour. It is a matter of timing, and this indicates a thicker mix, which is good for this type of cast as it will move slowly and if there are any leakages you have time to act. A thinner mix will run more freely and is often used if there is fine detail to cast. Pour the plaster in a smooth, steady manner, making sure it spreads out evenly into the mould, and tap the table with your fist to agitate the liquid slightly and force any air bubbles to the surface.

When the plaster sets, or 'goes off', it will heat up because of a chemical reaction, but once it has cooled, the cottles can be removed and the plaster panel can be slid to one side to release it from the glass. Sharp edges and corners can be trimmed with a surform blade, and a damp sponge can wipe away any clay residue. Let the blocks dry out thoroughly and evenly, placing them on wooden blocks or a wire rack so the air can circulate.

An alternative method for mixing plaster involves measuring out the water and plaster before you start. The recommended plaster-to-water ratio is 1½lb (680g) plaster to 1 pint (710ml) of water, and this amount can be multiplied to make larger quantities.

SPONGE STAMPS

Sponge printing is the ideal method for creating repetitive patterns. This traditional ceramic technique uses blocks of sponge or textural natural sponges to print pigment, glaze or wax. Their flexibility and absorbent qualities mean they can hold the colour and will print with ease. The surface texture of the sponge and the type of colour or pigment used will dictate the quality of the print. There is a variety of polyurethane sponges available, but a smooth, dense type will yield the best results and will achieve a defined image. Upholstery sponge, which should be at least 1.5in (3.8cm) thick, or the large block-type sponges used by decorators, are suitable. The washing-up sponges that have a scourer on one surface are often used by my students: they are slightly softer and are easily available.

The sponge stamps can be used directly, printing a surface with slip, underglaze colour, oxides or glaze and producing the opposite image to the wax-resist prints. They can also be used to print pigment on to plaster when using paperclay or on to newsprint for the paper-transfer technique.

Making up plaster slabs of different sizes has proved to be very useful for a variety of decorative techniques, and a vital piece of equipment for the studio.

Smooth upholstery sponge or washing-up sponges are ideal to use for printing techniques, as they will print evenly.

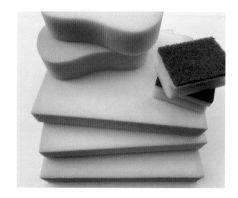

Direct printing with underglaze colour on to a leather-hard dark clay, using a selection of sponge stamps.

Sponge-printed decoration with wax resist, part of the author's 'Tension Visuelle' collection of wearable sculpture. (PHOTO: RICHARD KALINA)

SPONGE RESIST

This resist technique uses slip, underglaze colour or glaze with a water-based wax emulsion, and resembles batik, an ancient wax-resist dyeing method used on fabric. To prepare the stamps, the sponges can be cut into different sized blocks, drawing the patterns on the surface with a permanent marker, or designs can be drawn on the sponge first and then cut to size.

The most effective way to incorporate the design into the sponge is to melt it with a heated soldering iron, using a fine nib. Be aware that it is *very important* that the fumes are not inhaled, so there must be adequate ventilation; I would advise wearing an FFP3 mask, and the process should be done outside. (More information on masks can be found in Chapter 2.)

Once heated, the soldering-iron nib will engrave very easily into the surface of the sponge. Trace the design, creating deep linear marks, or burn away the background to leave a solid

The wax-resist technique uses sponge stamps and water-based wax with underglaze colour, and resembles the art of batik printing.

The engraved images on the sponge are made using a soldering iron, and simple designs yield the best results, but there is scope to experiment.

Painting a layer of contrasting colour into the unwaxed areas of each design will start to reveal the detail of the patterns.

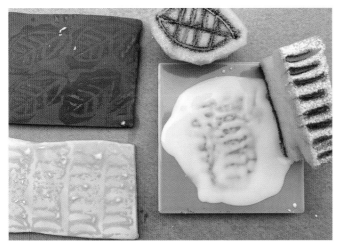

Printing the surface of the clay with an even pressure will achieve a consistent coating of wax from the stamp.

During the firing the wax burns away, but it leaves behind a printing quality in the colour that is exclusive to this technique.

shape. The smooth surface of the sponge that has not been etched away will be the area that will print.

This technique will work on leather-hard clay or a biscuit-fired surface, but the same process is used regardless of the stage of the making or what materials are being used. A layer of colour can be applied first and allowed to dry until it has a matt appearance: it is then ready for the wax. A glazed tile can be used as a palette, with a small quantity of the wax and a dash of water, spreading the mixture out over the tile. A little food colouring can be added to the mix to help keep track of the printing. Using a tile rather than a bowl or shallow dish of

wax ensures that the sponge is not swamped with liquid, and prevents flooding the surface when printing. This should also be used if printing with colour or glaze. In each case the sponge stamp should be rinsed with water before use and squeezed out thoroughly as this helps to achieve a successful print.

Dab the surface of the sponge stamp into the wax several times, making sure it is evenly coated, and apply the stamp to the clay surface, pressing firmly, replenishing the coating of wax for each application. All sponges and paintbrushes must be thoroughly cleaned in water after printing, as the wax will set and ruin them if left to dry.

If the print is not perfect, any details missing can be added using a paintbrush, and any unwanted wax can be scratched away. Allow the wax to dry thoroughly before applying a layer of a contrasting colour with a brush, directing it to the unwaxed areas, and avoid brushing across the whole area. There will be little droplets of colour that will appear on the wax, and these can be lifted off with a wet brush. They can also be left, as most will come away when the wax burns off, though some will fix on to the surface.

LASER-CUT STAMPS

An alternative way to make stamps is to use laser technology to engrave the shapes. It can produce precise and intricate designs, with the advantage of being able to repeat any of the stamps with the exact same design. The patterns can be compiled in drawing editing software, which will allow you to edit the images, adjust the scale and repeat patterns. The final designs for the stamps can be grouped together in one file, so they can be cut out together.

For this method, the designs were hand-drawn in black pen on paper and the images scanned, before they were converted into a vector file. Most companies who offer a laser cutting service also have designers and in-house drawing services that can help to translate ideas from paper, or convert digital images into the appropriate vector or CAD files. The material available that can be cut this way and is suitable for laser printing, is a smooth sheet of low odour rubber: this has a much firmer surface than sponge so will work well on a biscuit-fired piece, which has the porous quality to help transfer the colour. They will also work well printed on to newsprint, and can be used in the paper transfer technique. Trying them out on paper first will enable you to practise and get the right amount of colour to transfer. They can also be pressed into soft clay to create a low relief embossed design.

When the stamps are new they seem to have a sheen on the surface that resists any application of colour, so they can be lightly sanded with a fine wet-and-dry sandpaper or rubbed with a kitchen scourer, and this will remedy the problem. The most effective way to apply colour evenly on to the stamp ready for printing is to use a thin layer of sponge, cut from a washing-up sponge and coating the sponge with colour, using a brush so it can be used like an ink pad. The sponge section should be damp, and then a generous layer of underglaze colour should be applied with a brush. The stamp is dabbed lightly on to the colour several times, if needed, to get an even coverage, but being careful not to swamp it.

Colour will attach itself to the background, but this should not come in contact with the paper or clay during printing. However, some edges may appear in the print, and this can be reduced if more of the background is cut away with a sharp

The completed drawing has been converted into a vector file with the areas in black indicating where the rubber will be left after etching.

The rubber stamps have been cut out into sections, mounted on to small blocks of wood to make them easier to handle.

Testing out the rubber stamps on paper first will allow some practice with the application of underglaze colour before printing on to clay.

scalpel. Depending on the colour, the density of print may vary, so the application can be built up by carefully painting another layer of colour on to the design with a fine brush.

PAPER RESIST STENCILS

Paper is the perfect material for masking and making stencils, as it can be cut or torn into a variety of shapes to resist a coating of slip or washes of pigment. This method is very popular with students and professional makers alike for its simplicity and low-tech approach. It does, however, have great potential to create sophisticated surfaces, and many interesting effects can be achieved by using multiple stencils to create patterns, resulting in shallow relief and overlapping images. It is helpful if the paper can soften and stretch a little on the damp clay, which helps it adhere to the surface and achieve a precise graphic image. A slightly different approach is needed when working with glaze or pigment on a biscuit-fired surface; details of these techniques are featured in Chapter 8.

Newsprint is the perfect choice for this method as it is easy to cut, and shapes well when wet. Simple, bold designs work well and are graphically more effective, but remember it is possible to create positive or negative shapes. This means the slip can be painted inside the cut-out shape or round the outside of the paper shape. To create stencils, work on a cutting mat and use a new blade if using a scalpel or craft knife. The soft-grip craft knives that have a rotating blade are a valuable tool when it comes to cutting stencils, as they can create curved, meandering cut lines with ease.

Make sure the clay is leather hard, and smooth the surface with a firm rib before applying the first layer of slip if a colour is required under the paper rather than just the bare clay. This can also be a white slip, as this will ensure a perfectly smooth surface to work on. When the shine has gone, mist the stencils lightly with water, position the stencils on to the clay, and dab them firmly into place with a damp sponge or the fingertips, taking extra care with the edges of the design.

Paper is the perfect material to create a stencil, and potter Georgie Gardiner applies these to the clay surface, taking care they are firmly in place.

Apply even, thin layers of slip to ensure a smooth surface, and allow each one to dry before applying the next coat: it may take several layers to achieve the correct density. More paper stencils can be added to the design at this stage using a different colour, which becomes the background. Allow the slip to harden enough so the shine has gone before carefully peeling away the paper stencils to reveal the pattern. It may be helpful to use a blade to hook up a corner and start the peeling process without damaging the design.

Georgie Gardiner and her Use of Paper Resist Stencils

A simple paper stencil is the perfect way to introduce clean-cut edges and bold, graphic shapes into a design. This technique has the ability to create a more complex and sophisticated surface. Potter Georgie Gardiner's work has managed to achieve all that, by building up a layered design using leaf shapes and curved linear stems with different coloured engobe slips.

She has made the simple process of cutting paper stencils into a fine art, creating distinctive and elegant pieces. She chose to use paper resist on her thrown vessels as she was drawn to the potential for clean-cut edges and block colours, realizing it was the technique she wanted to explore and develop. It can take her months to cultivate a new design, and it is only through the process of doing, rather than drawing, that new directions become apparent. 'Paper behaves differently on a three-dimensional surface than on a flat one, but these challenges are the reason I keep coming back to it.'

Georgie has always been drawn to matt surfaces and didn't want to use glaze, so she experimented with engobes until she found a recipe that worked for her. The challenge is still about applying the right amount: too thin and it's patchy, but too thick and it bubbles. She applies her engobes with a brush, gradually building up the thickness over four to five coats, allowing each coat to become touch dry first as this helps to create a smooth surface without thick brush marks. Georgie uses three different white clays, one for her larger vessels, one for her bowls, and a semi-porcelain for the mini vessels.

Step 1: Apart from the semi-porcelain pieces, she will brush on several coats of white engobe before starting to apply the paper. This is to create a smooth white canvas without any faint turning marks.

Step 2: 'I want my forms to be free of any throwing rings or slight turning marks as I think that fights with the surface decoration.'

Step 3: She achieves her layering of leaves by applying the paper stems and some of the leaf shapes to the vessel, painting the whole piece a light colour, a pale grey for example.

Step 4: Another layer of paper leaves is applied, and these will appear to be in the background; she paints the whole surface a contrasting darker colour.

Step 5: The layers of paper are then peeled away to reveal the bold, graphic images, and after firing the pieces are sanded to create a smooth, tactile finish.

Step 6: The forms are the vital element for Georgie, but she says '...trying to achieve a harmonious balance between the form and decoration is what keeps me making.'

Georgie enjoys the challenge of working with paper stencils on a curved surface and creating clean-cut edges and block colour.

1

To create one of her designs, Georgie starts applying the first set of paper stencils on to a shallow dish, which has been painted with a smooth white engobe.

2

Before she starts to paint, Georgie plans the second layer of stencils, making a note of the positioning, then puts them aside.

3

Having painted several coats of a pale grey engobe over the paper stencils, she presses the next layer of paper cut-outs into position.

4

Georgie applies the second engobe slip over the whole surface, using a dark colour that will become the background.

5

Once the slip has dried to a dull sheen, she then carefully peels away the paper stencils to reveal the design, which is a very rewarding part of the process.

6

No need to use a glaze, as the layers of engobe, defined by the cut-out paper designs, produce dynamic results.

DRY CLAY TECHNIQUE

Stencils can be applied more freely on to a bone-dry surface using underglaze colours in a creamy consistency, or they can be diluted slightly, resulting in a watercolour-type effect. The stencils can be hand cut in newsprint, they can be positive and negative shapes, and it is worth having a selection to experiment with.

Taylor Sijan specializes in decorating her work using layers of newsprint stencils, building up the colours in a spontaneous way.

A selection of hand-drawn stencils that have been hand cut out of newsprint, utilizing both the positive and negative shapes.

The stencil is held in place with the fingertips on one edge, and a layer of colour is painted over the paper using a soft flat brush, painting along the centre of the shapes. The application of colour will help to grip it to the surface, holding it in place so additional layers can be applied. This process can be repeated several times over the surface, adding more paper stencils, overlapping them and varying the colour. Using a painterly approach with the design will ensure the different areas of colour are less defined and can blend or graduate together. If the stencils are difficult to keep in place, a light misting with water or a few dabs of a damp sponge will help. It is important that the layers are kept light, and building up the colour slowly will prevent the bone-dry surface from being swamped.

Taylor Sijan and her Use of the Dry Clay Technique

Taylor Sijan is an American artist based in Lincoln, Nebraska. She has embraced this method of decoration, and can achieve very luscious surfaces with her layers of stencils and underglaze colour. Part of her research as a graduate student was to develop complexities in her surfaces, and to develop her career as a

One of Taylor Sijan's painterly plates, where she has created depth to the layers, inspired by her love of plants.

Taylor creates her stencils by manipulating the designs in Adobe Illustrator, which are cut out using a laser cutter.

Taylor starts the process by building up layers of the newsprint stencils using a range of the lighter underglaze colours.

The darker colours are the last to be applied, just over sections of the plate and using more stencils.

studio potter without relying on a large outdoor kiln. Taylor had spent several years previously creating variety and depth in her work using wood and soda firings. She describes her approach and the decorative processes she has started to develop:

> Layering visual or tactile information at different stages in the making process is the key to achieving a richness in an electric kiln. In such a stable environment, a maker must intentionally layer techniques and materials to achieve complex effects. As a result, my decoration process has grown increasingly complicated and takes place at the freshly thrown, leather-hard, bone-dry and bisque stages.

Taylor stamps and slip trails her work while it is soft, and carves and refines it when it is leather hard. She paints layers of underglazes only after the porcelain is bone dry to avoid cracking due to uneven drying. During painting she creates a collage with the stencils of various plants, and builds up layers of colour strategically on sections, to create movement around the piece and to add focal points for the viewer. She makes her stencils by manipulating photographs or drawings of plants in Adobe Illustrator to create silhouettes that are cut out with a laser cutter. The stencils are made of newsprint paper because they need to soften and become pliable when wet, so they will stick to the surfaces of unfired and often curved pottery forms.

Once the shine has gone from the applied colour, all the paper stencils can be peeled away from the surface.

As she blends the underglazes across the form she will add more and more stencils while working from light to dark.

Since so many of her forms have curved surfaces, Taylor paints a layer of underglaze first, adds a dry stencil, and then paints over it using the same colour. This fixes the stencil in place and prevents any bleeding of underglaze around the edges of the stencil. She can then safely paint a layer of a different colour over the stencil, without compromising the edges of the images. After all the stencils are removed, she uses carving tools to refine the edges of the underglaze sections so that they have a crisp, sharp finish.

After all the stencils are removed, Taylor uses carving tools to refine any detail and tidy up round the underglaze colour.

The glazing process softens the details, which allows the colours to blend and melt together, giving the surface a luscious quality.

Finally she adds a few hand-painted details, and at this stage they are biscuit fired so she can continue layering with oxides and glazes before the final firing.

The glazes she uses soften the underglaze layers, blending them together slightly, and allowing the cobalt and copper oxides to pool and blend. She says of this process: 'The result of all this layering appears like fortuitous kiln magic, more spontaneous and less calculated than it was to achieve.'

TYVEK STENCILS

This waterproof material is used across many industries, and because of its durability, will make robust stencils that can be reused extensively. It can be easily cut with scissors, and delicate detail can be cut out with a scalpel or a precision craft knife. It is important to use a sharp new blade and to change it regularly because of the fibrous quality of the material. This material can also be used with a digital stencil cutter, and clean, precisely cut images will be produced from drawings or digital downloads.

The design can be drawn freehand in pencil or with a fine marker on to the Tyvek; another option is to make a tracing

Tyvek paper can be used in a digital stencil cutter, with the added advantage that a design can be repeated or adjusted in size and scale.

from a sketchbook idea, or even to print an image on the paper, using an ink jet or laser printer.

Stencils will work well on a dark clay or a white body in combination with a contrasting slip, when the clay is leather hard and has a smooth surface. The Tyvek stencils are put in a shallow tray of water in preparation, to soak for a few minutes, but dab them in a sheet of paper towel just before they are applied to the clay to absorb some of the excess moisture. A stencil can be placed directly on to the bare clay using a

When the Tyvek paper is digitally cut to create the positive shapes, there is the option to utilize the negative paper sections for decoration.

Tyvek paper stencils can be placed under slip to mask the surface, or placed on top of the slip, wiping the slip away around the stencil shape.

Two completed versions of applying a white slip on a dark clay body using Tyvek paper stencils, creating a dramatic contrast of negative and positive shapes.

damp sponge, to press it into place. A soft rib can then be used to compress it firmly, squeezing away any residual water, and making sure all the edges of the stencil are inlaid into the surface of the clay. Slip is painted over the whole area to create an even and opaque quality to the surface. It may need two to three coats, allowing each layer to dry to a dull sheen before applying another.

Alternatively, two layers of slip can be painted on first, but just in the area where the stencil will be placed. When the slip has lost its shine, the stencil can be positioned in the middle of the slipped area and pressed firmly into place as before. The excess slip around the stencil is wiped away with a clean sponge, which is rinsed regularly to keep the clay surface clear. If there is any grog in the body and the wiping action has created a textured surface, it can be compressed back into the clay with a soft rib. The stencils are removed from the clay to reveal the positive and negative shapes.

PAPER TRANSFER TECHNIQUE

The paper transfer technique resembles making a monoprint, which is one of the most straightforward methods of printmaking. Instead of drawing on a smooth and non-porous surface, the image is created on newsprint with coloured slips or underglaze colours and then transferred on to a smooth surface of leather-hard clay. As with all monoprints, the images created will be reversed, so keep this in mind if text is included in the design, as it will need to be drawn backwards, and the first

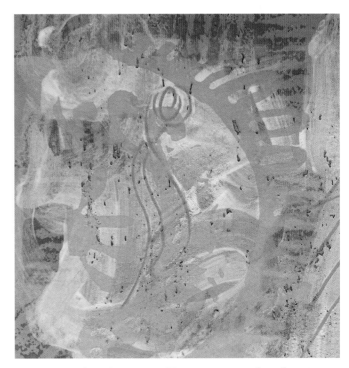

The paper transfer technique resembles a monoprint, with similar options for mark making using underglaze colours.

layer of colour applied to the paper will be the one revealed in the transfer. Any colour applied over the top of that initial layer will not be seen. Newspaper will work reasonably well, but newsprint is more durable, and is strong enough to hold and transfer the layers of slip. This technique will also work using a cotton cloth instead of paper as the transfer material.

A clay-based decorating slip can be used for this process, and can be applied generously to the newsprint in painterly blocks or intricate patterns, using different colours. Use brushes of different sizes, or try printing areas with sponge stamps.

A block of plaster can be used to work on, as this will help to absorb the moisture and will help the slip to dry evenly; because of the clay content, it will take longer to dry. Allow the shine to go until the slipped surface has a suede appearance – if it is too wet it will tend to squelch. Make sure the clay panel is nearly leather hard, and apply the painted paper face down on to the surface using a wooden roller or plastic rib to compress and transfer the colour from the paper to the clay. Lift a corner of the paper carefully to see if the transfer is working: if colour is still left on the paper, it can be placed back down again, compressed with a roller, or pressed firmly with the fingertips for a more complete transfer.

Nicola Gladwin and her Use of the Paper Transfer Technique

Nicola Gladwin has used a variety of decorative techniques over the years but has found that the painterly quality of the transfer technique perfectly suits her approach to decoration. Nicola, originally from Britain, has lived and worked as a potter in the depths of rural Brittany for the last thirty years and is inspired by the traditions of the French country potters. She says of her work:

Pottery has the possibility to outlive many generations, so it is important to me that each piece serves its purpose to the best of my ability and is also a pleasure to look at and use. The enjoyment of using something unique can bring back the memories of when it was bought or gifted, something you never get with a mass-produced item.

Her functional work is predominately thrown, using red earthenware, which is raw glazed. She uses several different techniques: pouring, slip trailing, sgraffito, sponging and most recently, paper resist and transfer. Her latest work has been based on the countryside where she lives: 'I love watching our chickens and ducks and the wildlife all around. The graphic images are used to represent the creatures, not as a replication of the real thing, but of their essential qualities.'

Nicola initially used her watercolour paintings as reference, aiming to recreate that painterly quality in her ceramic vessels, but she has also started to use her sketchbooks more, and the results have filtered down to decoration that she uses on her work.

She uses a ball clay to make her slips with a percentage of either oxides or high temperature commercial stains. Sections of the vessels are painted with black slip for creating incised

Nicola Gladwin's work reflects the local countryside, with graphic images of birds and flowers, aiming to show some of their essential qualities.

Nicola Gladwin uses her watercolours as reference, with the intention to recreate a painterly quality to the images she translates onto the clay.

detail at the end of the process, then they are dipped in white slip and allowed to go leather hard. She starts the transfers by slip trailing the outline of her designs on to newsprint using a dark blue or black slip, waiting until the surface has become matt, and then adding layers of coloured slip to complete the image.

The painted image is then transferred on to the clay, stroking with a rubber kidney to make sure that most of the image has transferred. As she peels away the paper, fragments of the design are often left behind, creating a distressed quality to the print – but she likes that.

More recently, Nicola has started to apply paper stencils on top of the transferred colour, sponging black slip into the shapes to create the graphic silhouettes of the birds and chickens, then adding a few slip-trailed details. When the work is still leather hard, she glazes the work using the same process as she does when dipping in slip.

Nicola initially slip-trails the outline of her design, adding coloured slips on a panel of newsprint, ready to transfer to the dish.

Nicola Gladwin has a very painterly approach to her designs, and this transfer method is the perfect technique to use.

Nicola has slip-trailed a leafy design, then added background colour on to the paper, transferring the image on to a painterly surface.

She has introduced cut-out paper stencils over the transferred image, ready to sponge black slip into the shapes.

Black slip has been added to highlight the embossed detail on the rim, and Nicola has added a few slip-trailed details to the birds.

Nicola raw-glazes her work, which has brought out the vibrancy of the colours and finally revealed all its painterly qualities.

Using Liquid Underglazes

The commercial liquid underglaze colours are ideal for this transfer technique as they are easy to use and come in a wide range of colours. It is possible to apply a more illustrative approach, create a painterly surface or print images in layers. However, this type of underglaze colour does not work well on its own as it contains binding agents and medium, which makes it difficult to transfer the colour from the paper. It is important to use the all-purpose slip (the recipe can be found in Chapter 4) or something similar, as this will act as a releasing agent for a successful transfer and will also dry faster than the clay-based slips.

Making Transfer Sheets

The great advantage of using liquid underglaze colours on newsprint is that if they are left to go completely dry, the decorated sheets can be kept and stored away for future use. I use the rougher, heavier newsprint for this method, and cut or tear it into A6 size – 4 × 5.8in (105 × 148mm) – sheets, but this can also be done on a larger scale. A few individual underglaze colours can be painted separately on to the A6 sections of the newsprint with a soft flat brush, covering the whole surface. Make sure the layers of colour are even – aim for about two coats, but make sure it is not too thick as it will start to crack or flake off in places.

Painterly and Printed Images

To create a variety of patterned sheets, different colours can be applied in many ways, using the printing techniques featured in this chapter. The underglaze colour can be applied using sponge stamps and constructed stamps, especially the offcuts of lino printing blocks. Colour can be smeared or painted through commercial stencils, or ones that have been made with a heated stencil cutter on the stencil sheets, or just with paper cut-outs. I found during my experiments that applying some colour on to the plastic sheet of the stencil, and pressing that on to the paper before painting colour through the spaces, produced some interesting transfer marks. This would be the perfect opportunity to try out laser-cut rubber stamps, as they are made of a firmer material and will print well on paper.

Allow each layer of colour to dry before you apply another, preventing them from blending if a sharper image is required. Additional layers can also comprise gestural strokes with a stiff brush in a contrasting colour; these can overlap the existing images and create the background. If there are gaps left on the paper, more printed or painted colour can be added – but remember, the first colours that come in contact with the surface of the paper will be seen when they are transferred. These sheets can be very experimental and not composed, as they can serve as collage sheets that can be cut up, edited and rearranged before being applied to a clay surface.

A collection of newsprint transfer sheets that have been decorated with underglaze colours, and which can be kept as a creative catalogue for future use.

The results can be a surprise when a layered print is transferred on to the clay and the complete design is finally revealed.

Decorative slips that have a lot of clay content are usually not suitable for this method as they will start to disintegrate and crack away from the paper as soon as they start to dry out. However, if a generous spoonful of CMC, an organic polymer, is added to the slip, this will transform it into a functioning alternative. It comes as a powder so must be dissolved in hot water, and the solution needs to be quite thick, resembling wallpaper paste – as a guide I use about half a cup of hot water to about 8g of CMC.

Using the Transfer Sheets

The transfer sheets can be used individually to build up a patterned surface, incorporating a whole sheet, or shapes can be cut out or torn to create a collaged image. To transfer the image, a generous, even coating of all-purpose slip is applied to the whole area with a soft flat brush. To avoid smudging the colour as it dissolves, allow the first coat to lose its shine before applying a second coat. This slip will dry relatively quickly, but things can be speeded up with a heat gun. A plaster block can be used as a base when applying the slip, and if the edges of the paper are painted over, it will secure them to the plaster, so when using a heat gun, it prevents the paper from being dislodged by the hot air.

Take care not to dry them too much, but they can be rescued by spraying the back of the paper to revitalize them. As the paper is laid on to the clay, a damp sponge can also be applied to any area that has started to dry. A plastic rib or roller is used to compress the colour into the clay as before, and the paper is gradually peeled away to reveal the slip and colour transfer.

The transfer can also resemble a distressed surface, which can look like peeled paint. This may work better with single or simpler blocks of colour. When transferring the slip and colour, don't smooth over the whole surface, but press with the fingertips at intervals over the surface, lifting the paper to check how much of the colour has transferred until the desired effect is achieved. There may be colour that is lifting away from the surface after the paper has been peeled away, but this can be compressed back into the clay using a clean sheet of newsprint and a roller.

The paper is carefully peeled away once the print has been successfully transferred on to the clay, using plastic ribs and fingertips.

The painted slip can be transferred from the newsprint to the clay, creating a distressed texture, resembling a weathered wall or peeling paint.

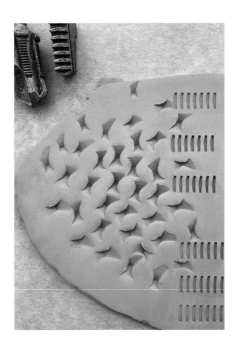

A soft panel of clay has been embossed with a pattern using found objects and then allowed to go leather hard before slip is applied.

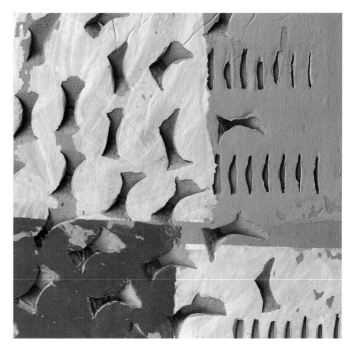

Panels of different coloured slipped paper are applied to an embossed surface and the colour only transfers on to the raised areas.

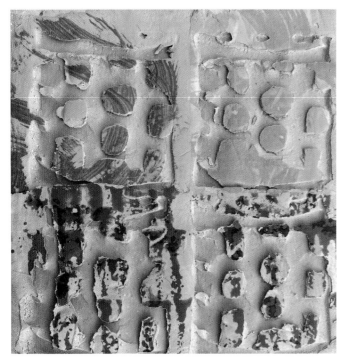

A sheet of patterned slip transfer has been applied to an embossed surface, leaving a defined pattern on the newsprint, which can be used independently.

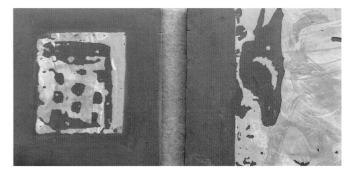

The slipped pattern left on the newsprint after a transfer has been applied to another surface to create an alternative pattern.

If the slipped paper is applied to an embossed clay surface, which has been created by pressing stamps into soft clay first, the colour will only transfer on to the raised areas. This also leaves a distinct pattern on the paper, which can be transferred independently on to another area or on to another sheet of clay. Let the embossed clay surface reach the leather-hard stage before applying any transfers, as the firmer surface will benefit the result of the printing.

WATER ETCHING

This resist technique is described in many ways by potters, influenced by the different resist materials they have used to achieve an embossed surface on raw clay. When the work is biscuit fired it burns away the resist material from the clay surface, revealing the design. Traditionally, wax or shellac was applied to the clay surface to create a design, and when the resist material had hardened, the surrounding clay surface was wiped away with a wet sponge to etch the background, leaving the embossed image intact. Because of the nature of the etching process, wax is often too fragile and will start to break up, especially if the design has delicate detail. Shellac is more robust – it can be painted or applied with a sponge, but it is quite runny, and the brushes and sponges will need to be cleaned in methylated spirits.

The more user-friendly resist materials to use are an acrylic varnish or a découpage glue and sealer such as Mod Podge. This gives more flexibility to the application as they are water soluble, which means they can be printed, applied with a sponge, or the design painted on to the clay with more control. This technique can be very effective on a smooth white body such as porcelain, and it can be left white, but other options are to use underglaze colour under the resist, or a tinted translucent glaze to accentuate the detail after it has been biscuit fired.

Textured or grogged clays can also produce some interesting results, and a dry wiping process can be explored on this type of clay, but it is advisable to wear a mask for this method. The resist material can be applied on a firm leather-hard surface, but also on bone-dry clay. Sponge stamps can be used to apply the resist, using a tile as a palette, which is the easiest way to coat the surface of the sponge evenly, ready for printing. It can be applied directly on to bare clay, or over a layer of colour that has been allowed to dry. If the design needs to be refined because too much resist has been applied, use a scalpel or sgraffito tool to scratch away any unwanted detail.

Whichever method is chosen to apply the resist, use a damp soft sponge to wipe away the background. Try not to use too much water, which may soften the clay too quickly; a gradual process is much more effective, but let it dry for a time during the process to recover, if needed. The application of colour can be also reversed, painting colour on to the background after the etching has been completed.

Steve Kelly and his Use of the Water-Etching Technique

American potter Steve Kelly has developed his own approach to the water-etching technique. He uses thin packing tape as his resist material, creating curvilinear recesses in his surfaces. He stretches lengths of tape in sections, creating curves and angles on to a bone-dry surface. This will ensure the tape adheres to the surface, as any moisture present in the clay would prevent this. His surfaces have an architectural quality, with typographical references such serifs, brackets and spurs. There is also a nod to his passion for American street art and the graffiti scene.

Steve wanted to create clean sharp edges to his designs on his thrown porcelain vessels, and found this technique to be the perfect solution.

A découpage glue has been painted through stencils, printed with sponge stamps over areas of colour, then etched away with water.

A water-etched vessel by Steve Kelly, who has a minimal approach to some of his pieces, choosing to leave the exterior surface unglazed.

Step 1: Steve uses panels of dimpled foam to support the bone-dry pieces as he works, and a variety of soft sponges to etch the surface.

Step 2: The packing tape is carefully applied onto the vessel, he doesn't cut the tape, but stretches it to create curves and angles on the surface.

Step 3: A clean damp sponge is applied to the exposed areas, wiping in all directions, rinsing the sponge out regularly in clean water and gradually etching the surface of the clay to create a defined, embossed surface.

Step 4: The tape is removed to expose the etching, and Steve will then apply the tape to another section of the vessel, to create more patterns to etch.

Step 5: The great advantage of Steve's technique is that all the tape is removed before firing, unlike the varnishes or wax often used for this method, which must be burnt off in the biscuit firing. The vessels are left to dry; during this water-etching process it is important to let the work recover and not get too wet, so as to avoid distorting the shapes.

Step 6: After the work has been biscuit fired, Steve will sand away any residual marks or imperfections with wet-and-dry sandpaper.

Step 7: Steve will choose glazes to accentuate and elevate the surface texture and design. He says: 'The glaze plays a supporting character, while the surface decoration is the protagonist.'

Steve uses panels of foam to support the work, plastic packing tape to create the designs, and sponges and clean water to etch the surface.

Packing tape is stretched into different angles and pressed firmly on to the dry surface, creating the shapes to be etched.

The exposed areas are wiped away with damp sponges, in different directions, rinsing with clean water at regular intervals.

The tape is removed from an etched area when it has reached the desired depth and the process is repeated on another section. (PHOTO: GREG KELLY)

The work is left to dry, but often Steve will work on several pieces at the same time, etching them in rotation to avoid any distortions.

Once the work has been biscuit fired, Steve will sand away any imperfections, making sure there is a perfectly smooth surface.

Steve chooses glazes that will accentuate the surface and pool into the detail and a translucent celadon glaze is one of his favourites.
(PHOTO: GREG KELLY)

The etching process has influenced his throwing style over time, and he has designed forms that he considers more receptive to the surface, and patterns that sweep the eye across the form.

PRINTING ON PLASTER

This technique resembles a monoprint, and is the perfect example of how adaptable such methods can be with the variety of marks that can be achieved, from the graphically bold to the very restrained. This approach uses a plaster block, and any delicate marks, colour or fragments of printing that are applied to the surface of the plaster will transfer perfectly. The absorbent quality of the plaster makes it the ideal material to explore painterly surfaces and experiment with printing techniques.

There are various ways to lift the patterns and marks made on the plaster, with liquid paperclay or casting slip. Both these methods involve a very wet application, and the images will transfer very easily. A soft sheet of clay can also be used, but will need a layer of slip to be applied to the clay first, to help lift the image. As the colours applied are relatively thin, they tend to sink into the surface of the plaster so a light misting of water over the plaster may also be needed. This may need a little practice, as the timing and consistency of the slip and colour needs to be managed. When using casting slip, a coil of

'Dash', a wall-mounted panel, part of the author's 'Circulus Collection', with printed oxide and crackle glaze on white earthenware.

Liquid porcelain paperclay has been poured over a freshly printed surface, using plaster cottle rings to contain the liquid clay.

'Vortex', a wall-mounted construction, part of the author's 'Circulus Collection', with printed underglaze colour on porcelain.

A large panel of plaster is used to create areas of printed pattern, which have been cast with liquid paperclay using metal cottle rings.

Cast panels of porcelain paperclay have been carefully peeled away from the plaster block to reveal their printed surfaces.

clay can be placed around the edge of the image and welded in place on to the plaster to create a wall to contain the liquid. This should be allowed to set and become a solid sheet, but still have some flexibility to make it easier to remove.

The liquid underglazes are ideal for creating patterns and marks in bright colours, but also to experiment with watery oxides and commercial stains. The colour can be applied in many ways. It can be painted, stippled, splattered, applied through stencils, or printed with sponge stamps. Liquid porcelain paperclay seems to be the most efficient material to use, as the paper content helps with the process and it picks up the finest details.

Paper stencils can also be used, cut or torn to mask areas. Other options are wiping out or distressing the colour with a finishing sponge, or scratching away colour carefully with a wooden tool. This will allow additional layers of colour to be applied over the top to fill in any spaces and to highlight marks or fine lines.

A selection of the author's printing experiments, using underglaze colours, stencils, and liquid porcelain paperclay.

'Dappled Blue', printed porcelain, sterling silver and rubber, part of the author's 'Tension Visuelle' sculpture to wear collection.
(PHOTO: RICHARD KALINA)

A generous layer of liquid paperclay is poured over the design and smoothed over with a palette knife or a rib, so the mixture is level. Allow the shine to go, and let it reach a nearly leather-hard stage, but still flexible, before attempting to peel it away from the plaster. Shapes can be cut out before removal, using a sharp knife or cutters, but avoid cutting into the plaster surface. As the printed layer is just on the surface, take care not to damage the print so take extra care when handling the finished fragments. Another option is to create the shapes as they are cast by using a metal or plaster ring as a cottle, pouring the liquid clay into the shape and leaving it to harden.

To create raised, embossed marks in the print, the surface of the plaster can be engraved with a sgraffito tool, taking care that the plaster dust is wiped away with a damp sponge, to avoid it getting into any clay or colour. Remember these are permanent marks that can be used again, but the plaster can be filed down with a surform blade and smoothed with wet-and-dry sandpaper to eradicate the design.

The amount of clay to use is flexible – applying it relatively thickly will result in a sturdy panel of clay, or using it thinly will result in wafer-thin fragments. Colour can be applied before casting, creating painterly detail, or the panel can be decorated with washes of colour or oxide after biscuit firing.

Keep in mind that the clay will shrink down as it stiffens, so it will be worth experimenting with the thickness. This can be adjusted, with more liquid clay smeared over the existing layers, or a fine serrated tool can scrape it back to even out or thin the layer. Two strips of wooden battening can be placed close to the outer edges of the plaster block on either side to help achieve an even layer of slip and to control the thickness, especially if working on a larger piece. A third strip of wood can be used as a levelling tool, held at an angle and dragged across the surface with the ends resting on the wooden strips.

Wendy Kershaw and her Use of Printing on Plaster

Scottish ceramist Wendy Kershaw creates intricate illustrations and has developed her own versions of this casting method on a plaster block, using fine porcelain or terracotta slips to create decorative panels. Wendy explains her precision-like process: 'I use clay to tell stories on porcelain in the form of wall panels, mounted cut-out flat shapes floating above a background, and books with movable pages. My narrative work illustrates poems, allegories and stories.'

Working on flat porcelain has proved to be a challenge, so to prevent warping, Wendy makes her slabs by turning the clay into a thick slip, and painting and pouring it on to a plaster bat, held in with thickness guides on each side and gum tape at the ends.

Wendy Kershaw makes her panels by turning the porcelain into a thick creamy slip and builds up layers on a smooth block of plaster.

One of Wendy Kershaw's narrative works, 'Windy Girl', skilfully made in porcelain; the profile is carefully cut out at the leather-hard stage.

Wendy Kershaw refers to the illustrative panels as 'Floating Work' and they represent poems, allegories and stories.

She uses a steel rule to level the top of the panel, and treats each side of the slab equally when drying, which is crucial to keeping them flat. The profiles of the 'Windy Girls' and other panels known as 'Floating Work' are carefully cut out at the leather-hard stage before a meticulous drying process. They are removed from the plaster, and dried between sheets and wooden boards on both sides, changing the sheets to help with the drying: at no time are they picked up by hand. When the clay is nearly bone dry, Wendy scuffs the surface with a metal sanding mesh (details about this abrasive material Abranet can be found in Chapter 2).

Wendy starts by sketching out her image with a very soft 8B pencil so as not to mark the clay, and the final design is painted on with blue food colouring so she can draw the lines into the clay with fine sewing needles. After biscuit firing, the surface is flooded with a mix of underglaze, stains and water, and this is rubbed over with a cloth to give the mid-tones. To get back to the white of the clay, large areas are washed back with a sponge, a pencil eraser cleans smaller areas, and a scalpel is used for the detail.

Layers of darker tones are built up with washes of the underglaze mix, and between layers Wendy distresses the surface with the metal mesh, creating fine white lines, the opposite of the dark lines that were laid down earlier in the raw clay, giving extra depth to the image. She fires to cone 6, and polishes with diamond pads and water to give a smooth surface.

Decals are applied next: Wendy uses stock decals for the flowers, butterflies and birds, but the face decals are made from her own artwork. Gold lustre is added to the surface and is fired to cone 014. Finally on-glaze enamel mixed with acrylic medium is painted on, usually for the hair, and again fired to cone 014. It is a time-consuming way to work, laying down the different layers over four firings, but it gives Wendy the images and surfaces she wants.

Although most of her work is in porcelain, she also enjoys painting porcelain slip on to terracotta slabs, which are made in the same way as her porcelain panels. She uses the sgrafitto technique to create the design, and removes the slip around the image, either with a flexible steel edge, with latex resist or water etching. The pieces are fired to cone 8, and polished. She explains the appeal of this clay: 'The thickness of the slip, and the brushstrokes used to apply it, are visible only after firing. There is a wonderful contrast between the white luminosity of the porcelain and the earthy, iron-specked warmth of the terracotta.'

Wendy also casts porcelain panels with an embossed image, which she has carved into a smooth panel of plaster. She draws the image with pencil first, then incises the lines directly into the plaster. What she draws as an incised line comes out in the clay as a positive, raised image and the deeper she draws into the plaster, the more embossed the design appears in the clay.

Strips of gummed paper are placed round the edge of the mould to hold the slip in place and act as a guide to thickness of the panel. Layers of the thick creamy slip are built up as before and allowed to go leather hard before the panel is carefully released from the plaster.

Wendy also works with a terracotta slip to create panels, as she loves the luminosity of the porcelain slip over the rich dark surface.

The smooth plaster block has been engraved with a design, and gummed tape applied around the edge of the block as a thickness guide.

Wendy paints or pours several even layers of the porcelain slip on to the surface until she fills the mould to the correct level.

When the porcelain slip has become leather hard the panel can be carefully peeled away revealing the embossed design.

Washes of an inky blue-black underglaze colour are applied to the panel to highlight the embossed detail.

Some examples of graphic images and drawings from the author's sketchbook transformed into silkscreen stencils.

The finishing on the panel consists of just the washes and cleaning away of an underglaze and water mix. Wendy uses two blues and a black underglaze, having done many tests of different proportions, to get the right inky blue-black. She uses the metal mesh both at the raw stage and after it has been fired. The scratched lines at the raw stage give dark lines, and the ones done after the biscuit firing and the application of the underglaze give white lines.

SILKSCREEN PRINTING

Screen printing is one of the most popular printing techniques, where a mesh is stretched over a frame and used to transfer colour on to a surface; traditionally this is on to fabric or paper, but it will also work well on clay. Essentially this printing method is a sophisticated form of stencil and involves pushing ink or colour through the screen with a squeegee on to the surface beneath. This technique may seem daunting as it can involve what seems a complicated process and specialist equipment.

However, there is a simple way to try this, using the traditional silkscreening technique but on a smaller scale, and it will still achieve a professional result. It uses a light-sensitive film without a silkscreen frame, and it just needs direct sunlight to expose the image. It is worth starting with a simple design to understand the process, and to have the opportunity to try out the printing with different applications of colour. A pre-coated emulsion stencil film that can only be opened in subdued lighting, is needed for this process, with an exposure board kit. More information regarding the equipment for this method can be found in Chapter 2.

The artwork must be a sharp, opaque image in black and white. It can take the form of text, graphic design, or a sketchbook drawing. The image can be adjusted in a Word document or a design program, and printed on to copier transparency film. The printer needs to be set on best quality or heavy ink volume to achieve the correct quality print needed. This service can also be carried out by your local print shop. Do not use paper as it needs to be transparent. The design can also be drawn directly on to the film using a high opaque marker, which is lightfast and waterproof. To act as a guide, the design can be placed under the film and traced. Lift it to the light to check there are no gaps in the black areas.

Once the artwork is ready, it can be set up with the exposure board kit to create the stencil. It is advisable to work in a dimly lit room throughout this part of the process, as the film you are using to create the stencil is light sensitive.

Making a Silkscreen Stencil

This simple approach to one of the most popular methods of printmaking offers the opportunity to produce a successful stencil with professional results, by just using sunlight.

Step 1: Place the prepared artwork on the clear acrylic sheet, the right way up.

Step 2: Cut the pre-emulsified stencil to size, allowing about a half an inch border around the artwork. Peel the protective backing from the stencil, discard this and place the exposed film shiny side down on to the transparency. Position the backboard with the felt side facing down and place it on top of the stencil and the acrylic sheet; secure them together with the bulldog clips on all sides. Turn it over, and your design at this stage will appear backwards. Place the panel of cardboard over the exposure unit to prevent any light exposing the stencil as it is placed out in the sun. Set a timer for one minute and place the unit in direct sunlight, and remove the cardboard panel to expose the film.

Step 3: Replace the cardboard panel when the minute is up to prevent overexposure. A cloudy or overcast day will not work as the exposure time will vary too much.

Step 4: Remove the light-sensitive film from the unit and submerge it in a bowl of cold tap water for fifteen minutes and a ghost image will appear. Soaking it longer will not harm the stencil. Gently agitate the film to remove the emulsion.

Step 5: Place the stencil on a sheet of plastic canvas to hold it steady, and rinse carefully on both sides, using a soft brush to remove any residue.

Hold the stencil to the light to check that the image is completely clear of any emulsion, as this is crucial to achieving a perfect print. Place the stencil between two layers of paper towel and gently pat it dry. Lay the stencil back on the plastic canvas and place it out in the sun for ten minutes to harden and dry the emulsion – this will make the stencil more durable and it will last longer.

The designs, created on the transparent film, are placed in the centre of the clear panel, making sure they are the correct way round.

The stencil film is placed on top of the design, clamped into place with the backing board and placed in direct sunlight for one minute.

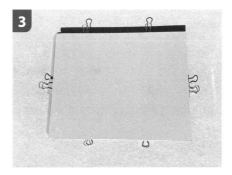

The cardboard panel is placed directly over the sunlight stencils after the correct exposure time to prevent any further exposure.

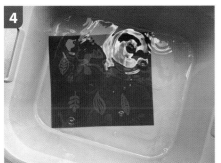

The stencils are soaked in a bowl of cold water for fifteen minutes to dissolve the emulsion from the ghost image.

A sheet of plastic canvas is used to steady the stencils, while washing away any emulsion residue with a soft brush.

The Printing Process

This method of printing can be used directly on to leather-hard clay; it works well on a biscuit-fired surface, and can be printed on to newsprint to use as a transfer. It does require a thicker viscosity to the pigment to guarantee a consistent and even transfer of colour for every surface. The commercial liquid underglazes will produce a clean, sharp print but will require some adjustment to the consistency to work correctly. This can be done by transferring the colour into a shallow bowl to allow some of the water to evaporate, which may take several days. If there are dried edges or thick skin that start to develop, stir it occasionally to help blend the mixture. A heavy medium or silkscreen medium can be added to prevent the colour from drying too quickly and clogging up the screen. Use about one part medium to two parts colour, but quantities may vary as different pigments may require different amounts.

Soak the stencil in water before you start printing. This should take about ten minutes, and allows the stencil to become more flexible and will help it to grip the clay surface. Dry the stencil between a couple of layers of paper towel to remove any excess water, making sure there is none trapped in the screen's mesh. If, however, the prints are being made straight after the stencil has been created, soaking will not be necessary.

Place the stencil in position on the clay surface and apply an even coat of the thickened colour with a sponge, stipple brush or use a rib to push the colour through. Alternatively, use fingertips to smear the colour into the area, which can be the best approach if working on a curved surface. It can produce precise graphic images, but if the colour can be applied in a more gestural way, this will affect how much colour comes through the stencil and will change the quality of the print.

Caroline Whitehead and her Use of the Silkscreening Technique

Caroline Whitehead has used her skills as a printmaker, and has also started to explore ways of echoing her ideas that she prints on paper, to print on to clay. She initially created monoprints, using a plaster block as the substrate, and porcelain paperclay to lift the prints. She revelled in the flexibility of the process compared to paper, and enjoys the opportunity to experiment.

She has now adapted her silkscreening technique by using an embroidery hoop, silkscreen mesh, paper stencils and a plastic rib to make prints using liquid paperclay.

Caroline prints her images on to a plaster block using liquid underglazes that have been combined with the organic binder CMC or a silkscreen medium to adjust the consistency. She prefers using the plaster surface as a substrate because it is so versatile and allows her to be able to manipulate and adjust the images, which is not possible when printing on to paper. The embroidery-hoop screens are very lightweight and easy to manoeuvre, allowing her to print multiple small images onto surfaces that would be awkward to print with a conventional screen. Caroline explains:

The small silkscreen panel has been used in a more abstract fashion, printing over colour on a leather-hard surface.

As a biscuit-fired surface is more absorbent, the colour sinks in more quickly, so there can be experiments with overlapping prints.

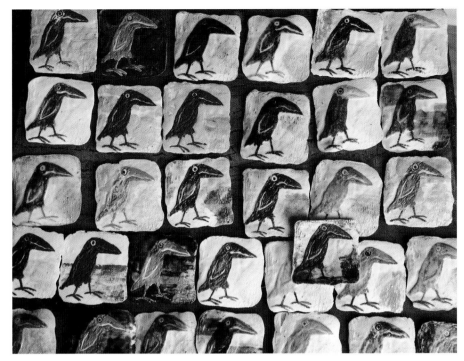

Small, printed panels in porcelain paperclay by Caroline Whitehead, using a monoprinting technique on to plaster, with underglaze colours.

One of Caroline Whitehead's prints on Japanese rice paper. Her ideas as a printmaker have influenced the imagery she has chosen to print on clay.

I'm not a traditional printmaker, because I get very excited when things go 'wrong'. To me, unexpected marks and misaligned layers of colour are magical, and this method makes such mishaps more likely. Because the underglazes and slips are opaque, there's no way of knowing the result until you peel the thin slab of porcelain away from the plaster. It's like glass painting, but without being able to look at the other side of the glass to see what's going on. I find this uncertainty very liberating.

Caroline's process can be very fluid and experimental as she paints directly on to the screen with a brush to create variations, before using the plastic rib as a squeegee, to pull a different colour across the screen to make the print. This allows her to print the same basic image many times but in many different variations.

Silkscreen Printing on to Plaster

Silkscreen printing on to plaster is extremely versatile as it allows for alterations to the images and the opportunity to adjust and add different details to the prints during the process.

Step 1: Once the image is printed on the plaster block, it can be altered by carefully scratching into the design and adding new colours to create detail.

Step 2: Additional colours can be applied at this stage, and Caroline will often overlap the images as she continues to silkscreen the images on to the plaster.

Step 3: Washes of colour or oxides can then be applied over the printed images to create a background. Caroline has chosen to add another stencil, a wavy motif that she prints over the birds.

Step 4: Finally, the plaster panel is covered with a generous, even layer of liquid porcelain paperclay. The absorbent quality of the plaster allows the paperclay to dry out enough so the whole panel can be peeled slowly away from the surface, with the printed images embedded into the surface.

Step 5: The panel is removed while it is still flexible, which makes handling easier, and it can be manipulated into a form if required. The firing intensifies the colours, and the casting process has highlighted the texture of the plaster surface flaws, which Caroline sees as a bonus.

Caroline prints her bird motif over the surface of the plaster and the smears and smudges can be cleaned or scratched away.

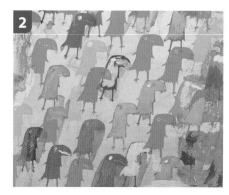

She continues the print with additional colours, adding detail, filling in with a contrasting colour and overlapping the images.

Caroline incorporates a second stencil and prints the wavy design over the birds to create a decorative background.

After a generous layer of liquid clay has been applied, the whole sheet was carefully peeled away from the surface to reveal the print.

The completed fired image on porcelain paperclay. Caroline's illustrative style works perfectly with this flexible printing technique.

Caroline will often cast small panels of porcelain paperclay to create individual prints, leaving the uneven edge.

Caroline sometimes applies the paperclay slip in small panels and mounts them in frames as she does with her works on paper, not cutting the edges, but leaving the panels as they were poured.

The porcelain is fired directly to stoneware, and sometimes raw glazed in sections to create contrasting effects. She has also experimented with using a fine dusting of talc on to the plaster surface before printing as this acts as a resist and can create speckles in the final print. Dust from grated colour sticks can be used in the same way and often the dust gets embedded in the screen mesh so will appear in subsequent prints.

Preparing the Screen

Caroline recommends using a coarse mesh such as 43T UK (110 US), which is traditionally intended for printing on textiles, the numbers referring to the thread count. A circle of mesh is cut, about 2in (5cm) larger than the embroidery hoop, and then secured as tautly as possible in the hoop. A circle of newsprint, slightly smaller than the hoop, is used to cut out the stencil shape from the centre, using a sharp scalpel. The design for the stencil should be the same size as the squeegee, so that one pull across with the colour will cover the stencil shape when making a print.

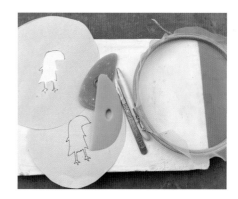

A home-made silkscreen, made from an embroidery hoop with hand-cut paper stencils and plastic ribs, serving as a squeegee.

The paper stencil is placed on the surface to be printed with four tabs of double-sided tape placed around the edges of the paper, and the embroidery hoop screen is then placed over the top. This helps to stop the edges of the paper lifting. A modest amount of colour is applied just above the cut-out image, and pulled across the screen with the rib held at a slight angle – this will grip the central part of the stencil to the surface of the screen as the colour is pushed through, holding it in place. To create a small gap between the surface being printed and the screen, referred to as the 'snap', thin battens of wood or strips of mount card are placed on either side, so the edge of the screen rests on these supports.

This enables the screen to be lifted away from the substrate immediately, which is important for obtaining a clean-edged print. Work quickly to prevent the colour from drying and blocking the mesh. Should this happen, take the stencil off, clean the screen with a wet sponge, and dab dry with some paper towel – the process can then start again.

Once the screen is set up, there is the opportunity to play with the application of colour, and to explore printing on plaster or paper, or directly on to a raw or a fired clay surface. All-purpose slip should be used on the paper prints to release

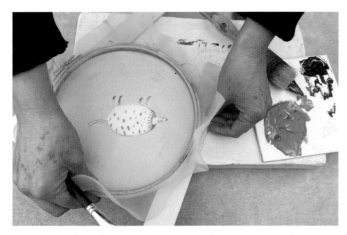

Slim battens of wood or mount card are placed under the edge of the screen before printing, to create a small gap known as the 'snap'.

The colour is applied to the screen and pulled across the image using a rib, held at a slight angle to ensure an even pressure.

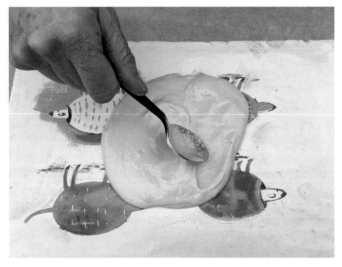

Porcelain paperclay is applied in generous spoonfuls and smeared over the plaster, creating a smooth and even layer over the whole design.

The final print is revealed after it has been peeled away from the plaster once the clay is leather hard, but still flexible.

the image from the paper, when transferring on to clay. If a coarser newsprint is used for the stencil, it will be more robust and should last longer – it can even be used again if allowed to dry out. A generous layer of liquid paperclay is applied over the completed print and allowed to go leather hard, before carefully peeling the cast away from the plaster.

DUST PRINTS

This technique uses bone-dry clay, pigment, or glaze used in a powdered form. It can be scattered or sieved, creating a decorative layer that is transferred on to soft clay, and the powder compressed into the surface. Just using a dark clay body dust printed on to a lighter clay, or the other way round, can be very effective. There is scope to use a variety of materials, which can be combined, so a wonderful opportunity for experimenting.

The dust can be applied directly to the clay using fragments of paper or stencils to create a pattern. The image, however, will need to be inlaid into the surface using a clean sheet of newsprint and a roller to compress the dust into the surface. A more flexible and gestural approach is to prepare the print on a dry, flat surface, a smooth wooden board or a table. Areas can be masked with stencils of any kind or torn paper, and additional linear marks can be engraved into the dust with a variety of tools. A contrasting colour can be sifted over the exposed areas for added detail – the colour sticks featured in Chapter 4 are an ideal material to use for this. These blocks of dried, compressed coloured clay can be grated using a domestic sieve to create the dust. Wear a mask throughout this procedure as you are dealing with very fine particles that are easily airborne.

A soft sheet of clay can be placed carefully over the image once all the stencils have been removed; then using a rolling pin over the back, compress the dust into the surface. If you are using clay or glaze for this method, to prepare this material it should be bone dry and ground to a fine powder in a pestle and mortar, or use a rolling pin, rolling over the material in a sturdy plastic bag. The powder should then be sieved using a domestic sieve and stored in an air-tight container. Oxides and commercial stains are already in the correct condition to use, so no preparation is required.

Catherine White and her Experience with Printing with Dust

Printing with dust is such an elemental notion, and American potter Catherine White's experience with developing this method certainly illustrates that. She describes her fascination with the technique, and her discovery of creating such a surface that can evoke memories and inspire significant meanings:

> The dust prints began as a way to find beauty and intrigue in the cooler, less ashy middle floor section of our anagama wood kiln. I began by thinking about how historically potters invented glaze. I imagine that ancient Chinese potters, after studying the accumulation of melted ash on the shoulders of jars, chose to add some ash before the firing. Evidence of this can be seen on some Han Dynasty jars. I began experimenting with ways of getting ash on to the pots that were to be stacked on our sandy kiln floor. My solution was to impress the ash on to the wet clay during making so that it would melt and create markings after firing.

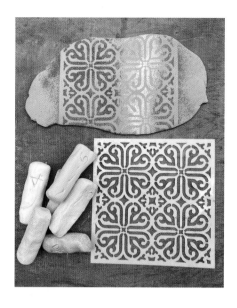

The dust-printing technique, using grated colour through a commercial plastic stencil, directly on to damp clay.

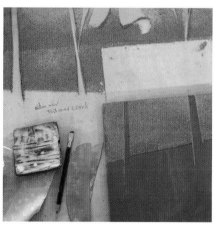

Catherine is fascinated by the dust-printing technique, and has developed this method through her experiments when firing her anagama wood kiln.

Creating Dust Images

Catherine White has developed a process of applying ash dust to her work so it would melt and create marks on the surface of the clay when fired in her anagama wood kiln. She uses her drawings and collages as reference throughout the process, measuring and drawing on the table in pencil before she starts. The dust images she creates will meander over a series of shallow dishes as a continuous narrative. She says of her choice of materials for the dust prints: 'For me, a minimal palette is liberating, enabling the touch of my hand as well as the visual lines and volumes of a shape to establish a physical texture of emotion.'

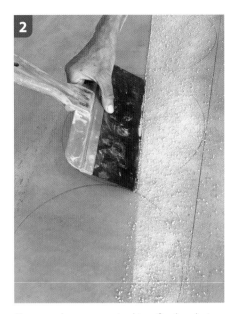

Catherine sieves a layer of ash on to the table, masking a section with paper, creating a long horizontal image. (PHOTO: WARREN FREDERICK)

She uses a large scraper tool to refine her design by tidying the edge of the dusted layer to ensure a sharp image. (PHOTO: WARREN FREDERICK)

A serrated tool is dragged through sections of the dust in a circular motion, creating linear marks and spaces in the design. (PHOTO: WARREN FREDERICK)

Step 1: Initially, thinking about horizon lines, Catherine used paper to create resists when she sifted the ash, creating the equivalent of an inked surface drawing. She used a long wooden worktable as the matrix.

Step 2: Using a wide scraper, she defines the edges of the dust and creates a sharp line.

Step 3: Catherine then engraves through the dust with a variety of tools, using her drawings as a guide.

Step 4: She also has a collection of metal rings that are used to achieve perfect circles into the dust along the print.

Step 5: After creating the desired ash pattern, she presses a series of wet clay slabs on to the ash with a rolling pin…

Step 6: …transferring a long horizontal image to become a set of clay plates.

Catherine has made many variations, each set exhibited or displayed on a long shelf to capture the essence of the horizon lines of a landscape.

After multiple cycles of making horizon-line series of plates, Catherine began to experiment with other vessels and different kinds of drawings with various materials. One current focus is using written text as a pattern. It often becomes unreadable, so it might be best described as asemic text. She prefers to work from the specific rather than the generic. Committed to using words with meaning, her sources range from published poetry excerpts to the personally evocative poetry she has drawn from archives of her mother's poems. With this heartfelt intention she finds the results expressive even as the marks become abstract or illegible.

The work 'Clay Pages' came out of experiments with wild materials such as local ochre, clays, and basalt rock dust. Each of the materials had beautiful colours in the raw state, but when fired in heavy reduction to high temperature, they lost much of their variation. Catherine had been looking at Chinese tombware, some of which was decorated with what is called 'cold slip' – fired pots with unfired slip. The colours were fantastic and had lasted thousands of years, so she decided to make thin, bisqued clay sheets so she could apply the wet raw materials to the absorbent surface. She explains:

4

Catherine uses an assortment of metal rings to use as templates to help guide the ash into graphic shapes. (PHOTO: WARREN FREDERICK)

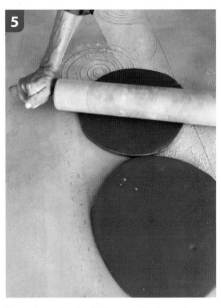

5

Several panels of soft clay are rolled over the length of the dusted image, embedding the marks into the surface. (PHOTO: WARREN FREDERICK)

6

The printed sections of clay are cut and curved over a hump mould to create a set of shallow dishes that echo views of the land. (PHOTO: WARREN FREDERICK)

From my experience with the sketchbooks, I love the way my marks get manipulated when printed. So I began brushing, painting or dipping paper in different slips, and then layering them on to the clay slabs. By immediately pulling the paper off, the slip is left behind. Remaining unfired, these clay pages are similar to a clay substrate with pastels.

Catherine has made many variations of her plates, and each set is exhibited on a long shelf to capture the essence of the horizon lines of a landscape.

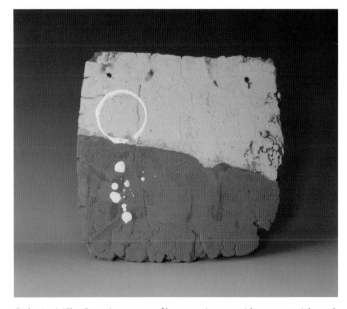

Catherine's 'Clay Pages' came out of her experiments with raw materials, and she chooses to leave the slips unfired to retain their vibrant quality. (PHOTO: WARREN FREDERICK)

CHAPTER 6

COLOUR IN CLAY

One of the joys of putting colour and often pattern through the clay body is the fact that each image will be unique, as this decorative process can introduce so many variations. Mixing pigment into any clay can offer the potter yet another wealth of possibilities regarding a decorated surface. One of its attractions is that the process presents the advantage of constructing and creating decorative marks simultaneously – when pattern, colour and form can be combined. The choice is often not to glaze the work but to develop a surface resembling a polished pebble with a combination of burnishing or sanding. A transparent glaze can be applied to enhance the colours, but there seems to be a preference to keeping a smooth matt surface.

Many of the techniques using coloured clay can be technically challenging and often take a great deal of time and effort to perfect. A whole book could be dedicated to the intricacies of mixing colour in clay, and the ways it can be used. I have included some more experimental methods that deal with applying coloured clay and pigment to the surface, which will hopefully act as a taster to tackling the more intricate methods.

Potters have adopted different ways to mixing colour into their choice of clay. It can be messy and time-consuming, but there are some methods that should help to minimize the mess. As to the time it takes, I think it's worth the effort. Starting with dry ingredients is generally considered more accurate, and to use a white clay body as the base, but there is no reason why there can't be experiments with adding colour or oxide to a tonally darker clay, as most clays can be stained. Using ceramic

Ceramic artist Judy McKenzie uses a wide range of ceramic stains to mix into porcelain clay, creating a vibrant palette for her Nerikomi pieces.

stains is a reliable option: they produce high intensity colours in slips, glazes, engobes and clay bodies. Most stains specify on the packaging the percentage required for achieving an accurate colour, which is usually 8–15 per cent (8–15g) of stain, for every 100g of dry clay. Experiment with smaller percentages of stain if a more subtle shade is required.

◀ The distinctive and painterly patterns in coloured porcelain are created by ceramic artist Judy McKenzie, using the Nerikomi technique.
(PHOTO: PAUL HAMMOND)

If using oxides to colour the clay, they should be used in smaller quantities, up to about 5 per cent – though even that may be excessive for some clay bodies, as they are very powerful pigments. Larger amounts may cause the clay to bloat or blister, as most oxides act as a flux and reduce the firing temperature of a clay. However, if a more distressed, textured surface is desired, just go ahead and test. There is some flexibility in adding more pigment or mixing different stains or oxides together – just make sure to document all experiments, and stick to the same method of measuring so it can be repeated.

Mixing the dry clay and pigment together in a sturdy plastic bag is an alternative method for mixing colour into the clay, helping to minimize the mess.

Water has been added and allowed to settle, and more dry clay is added to the mixture to ensure a more malleable consistency.

WHAT YOU WILL NEED

Digital scales are an important piece of equipment for preparing coloured clay, but starting a technical notebook is also crucial to keeping track of experiments. The clays I have listed are my preference, but feel free to test any clay body.

Equipment
- Digital scales
- 80-mesh sieve
- Small plastic buckets
- Plaster block
- Metal mixing bowl
- Rolling pin
- Wooden mallet
- Wooden spatula

- Plastic food storage boxes with lids
- Small food grater
- Stencils
- Plastic rib and metal kidney
- Long-bladed knife
- Water spray
- Permanent marker

Materials
- Porcelain or a white stoneware body
- Oxides or ceramic stains
- Liquid underglaze colour
- Resealable storage bags
- Cotton sheet – handkerchief size
- Disposable gloves

MIXING, TESTING AND STORING PROCESSES

Dry Clay
Weigh out the batch of dry clay, which has been broken down or crushed into small pieces, and divide it into two equal amounts, adding the percentage of powdered colour to one half of the dry clay, and place it into a resealable zipper storage bag.

Use enough warm water to cover the dry mixture, and leave it to slake down evenly for at least an hour. Add the other half of dry clay, and this can be left longer so that the dry clay can be absorbed into the mixture, eventually resulting in a batch of kneadable clay. Once it has dissolved, squeeze and manipulate the bag to create an even mixture.

The mixture can be left until it is firm enough to remove and wedge, so the bag can be left open if required. When it has reached that stage, decant the mixture on to a thin cotton sheet placed over a plaster block, by pulling the bag up and turning it inside out.

Turn the bag back the right way, as any residue of coloured clay left inside can be allowed to dry, and those fragments can be kept in the bag for other projects. The cloth can be used to get the clay into a manageable block and absorb any stickiness. Using the bags and the cloth will minimize the staining of the plaster and absorb the moisture of the clay, as it can be a messy business. A final wedge is made on the plaster before wrapping it in plastic, then it is put into a new bag, using a permanent marker to label each colour.

Plastic Clay

Weigh out a batch of clay, pat it into a block, and cut it into several even layers with a wire, like slicing a loaf. When using clay in this state, 30 per cent of the plastic clay is water, so allow for this or add 30 per cent extra clay.

Weigh out the dry pigment and add enough hot water to mix it into a smooth paste in a small container. Smear each sliced layer with the mixture, and stack the clay back together into a block; then wedge thoroughly until the colour has merged evenly into the clay. If any colour is left in the container use a piece of the clay to wipe up and absorb any residue.

Another option is to tear the clay into small pieces and place it in a large metal mixing bowl. The dry pigment is mixed with a little more water to create a slightly thinner mixture, and pour it over the clay pieces. Using hands and fingers, squeeze and mix the clay to blend in the colour. Finally, wedge on a board or a plaster block to get a good consistency. In both cases, when using plastic clay, it may be advisable to use disposable gloves. Using a metal bowl helps the mixing process due to the shiny surface, which tends to work better than plastic.

Testing

It is crucial that a sample or test piece is made of each coloured clay for reference. There is the option to glazing one section of the test in a transparent glaze, to compare a matt and a shiny surface. A shiny glaze can sometimes detract from a complex surface, but a clear glaze will usually intensify the colour – it's a matter of choice. It is useful to make two test pieces for each coloured clay, one to provide a reference in the studio, and the other to be stored with the batch of clay so the colours can be identified straightaway.

Storing

The consensus among some makers who work with coloured clay is to store the prepared colours for at least three months before using them to help mature the clay. This allows the stain to migrate right through and makes it more malleable. It seems that the longer it is kept, the better. The wrapped parcels of clay can be stored in plastic containers that stack easily. However, if you are keen to try out the colours, feel free to just go ahead and experiment.

Recycling

Keep all the dry scraps of coloured clay, separating the colours to recycle, or all the scraps can be combined and stained a darker colour or black. Recycling is an ideal opportunity to add other ingredients, so the testing and experimenting can continue.

JUDY McKENZIE AND HER USE OF COLOURED CLAY

Ceramic artist Judy Mckenzie produces very distinctive and beautiful painterly patterns by colouring porcelain and creating gradations of colour. She employs a practical method to mixing her colours and it can take up to an hour to mix and blend each colour. Her latest body of work employs a technique referred to as Nerikomi that originated in Japan and requires layering, cutting and blending different coloured clays together. This process ensures the colour and patterns go all the way through the clay, not just on the surface.

Judy explains her fascination with this technique:

Nerikomi embraces everything I love about working with clay. Every particle is worked by hand, from colouring the porcelain with stains and oxides, to forming patterns and creating designs. Patterns are embedded within the porcelain and become the DNA of the material from which forms can be manipulated. A dialogue ensues between maker and material. A design can be imposed, but the clay will distort and twist, giving rise to its own voice, creating its own unique patterns. Nerikomi is an ancient process but one which lends itself beautifully to reinvention. The endless possibilities for creating new patterns, colour combinations and forms are extremely exciting, and although the process is extremely time consuming, I find the whole process totally absorbing and the results very rewarding.

Mixing the Colour

Judy McKenzie has a practical approach to mixing the ceramic stains into porcelain clay, and a crucial part of creating patterns for her Nerikomi pieces is the meticulous mixing of each individual colour into a range of graduated shades.

Judy McKenzie has used the Nerikomi technique to create a beautiful surface with a palette of graded coloured porcelain.
(PHOTO: PAUL HAMMOND)

Step 1: Judy starts the process of mixing her colours by weighing out balls of clay (500g). She creates a pinch pot out of the weighed clay and places it back on the scales and sets it to zero. 50g (10 per cent) of stain is added to the well of the pinch pot.

Step 2: She adds a few drops of water at a time, mixing the colour into a thick paste.

Step 3: She is careful not to add too much water but makes sure all the powder has been blended into the mixture.

Step 4: Judy then kneads the ball of clay thoroughly, until all the colour is completely fused into the clay.

Step 5: To create the gradient of colour, Judy uses two blocks of coloured porcelain, both 500g in weight, that have been stained with different amounts of the same pigment. The lighter colour has 25g of stain, the darker has 50g of stain. She creates a tapered wedge or coil out of each block of colour and they are placed together, so the wider end is next to a thinner end, and pats them firmly together to make one cohesive block of clay.

Step 6: The block is divided evenly into sections, initially scoring with a knife along the block. They are cut off individually and each section is kneaded, combining the two shades of colour together. Each section is then rolled out on a smooth cotton cloth and then one is placed on top of the other, in the same order to form a block again. They are compacted together using the cloth, to cajole it into shape, so the edges of graded colour are quite visible, but now a smooth continuous blend of colour.

Step 7: Each prepared, graded colour is wrapped carefully and stored until Judy has a full repertoire of colours to construct her next collection of vessels. Each new batch of colours can take up to two weeks to prepare.

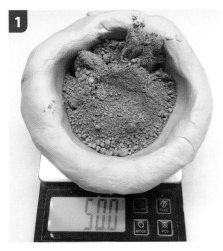

A pinch pot is created out of the weighed clay, which is a convenient way to add the right amount of pigment.

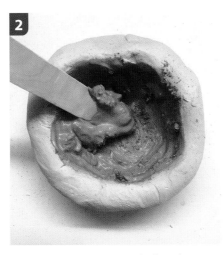

Drops of water are added gradually to the pigment and mixed thoroughly into a thick paste in the centre of the clay.

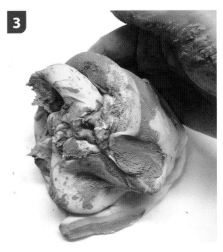

The clay is thoroughly wedged by hand, until all the colour has been blended into the body of the clay.

After wedging, the clay should now be a consistent colour throughout and ready for the next stage.

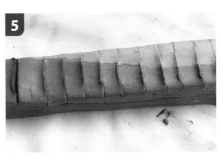

Two tapered wedges of clay, mixed with a different amount of the same colour, are placed end to end, so they can be sliced into sections.

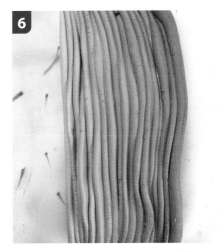

Each section is wedged, revealing the different graded tones of the colour, then rolled out and stacked together.

Judy spends time preparing enough blocks of graded colours, which are wrapped carefully in plastic, to make her next collection.

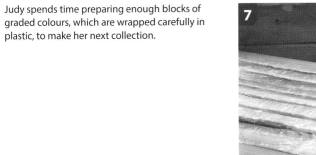

The Making Process

Judy McKenzie uses her palette of vibrantly coloured porcelain and manipulates the graded colours into painterly shapes, which are embedded together, creating a tall vessel. The work is refined and after firing, polished to reveal a sophisticated surface.

Step 1: Judy uses a variety of plaster moulds, which is an important part of her making process and in this case a two-part mould provides the form she wants.

Step 2: She arranges the coloured clays together, building up two decorative slabs of clay and then lays them into the sections of the plaster mould to construct the form. The two pieces of the mould are compressed together to make a complete vessel. Judy will also adapt this process depending on the form and will construct the coloured clay and the patterns, directly into mould. The clay structure is allowed to stiffen enough so the piece can be lifted out of the mould without any distortion.

Step 3: The next stage is to eradicate the seams and work on the surface to sharpen and refine the pattern.

Step 4: Once the work has been fired, the vessel goes through a long process of sanding to produce a beautifully smooth and tactile surface that will reveal the elaborate and painterly marks she has so painstakingly put together.

Judy uses plaster moulds to create her shapes and constructs the coloured clay into patterned sheets, before laying them into the two halves of the mould.

The edges of the clay panels have been compressed together inside the mould to create a complete form, which is revealed when the mould is carefully prised apart.

Tidying the seams and refining the surface takes time, but this process exposes all the decorative detail.

4

Judy's completed vessel, which has been meticulously sanded after firing, producing a beautiful, polished surface.

COLOURED GROG

Creating a coloured grog from stained clay is an alternative way to incorporate coloured clay into the clay surface, but in a fired state. It can give control over the range and tone of colours, and create a very different surface quality. Grog is a fired material that is often added to clays to help prevent warping and increase the resistance to thermal shock. This home-made version is used in a more decorative way, with the advantage of making different grades of particles to suit each project. The clay is prepared by rolling it out into sheets and allowing it to dry. It can then be broken up into small fragments using a rolling pin or a wooden mallet with a cloth over the clay to contain it.

It is advisable to wear a mask as this process can generate a lot of dust. Try not to pulverize it too much, especially if you have used thin sheets of clay – just enough so there is an assortment of manageable pieces, as it will break down into fine dust quite quickly.

All the crushed material can be placed in piles directly on to a kiln shelf and fired to around 900°C (1,652°F), and it will still be soft enough that it can be crushed easily to adjust the particle size. The grog can also be fired in biscuit-fired dishes to contain the fragments if preferred.

The grog can be wedged into the body of the clay or used as a decorative surface. Tests can be made by laying out the coloured fragments on to a plaster block and carefully spooning liquid paperclay over them to hold them in place. When the liquid starts to stiffen, a plastic rib can be moved over the

Homemade grog, made from coloured clays, fired directly on to a kiln shelf; all the fragments are carefully removed after the firing.

Liquid paperclay has been spooned over the coloured grog fragments, and a plastic rib is used to level out the surface.

The grogged panels have been fired and the colours have become more vibrant, and highlight the gaps and crevices created by the fragments.

Fired coloured grog has been embedded into a sheet of soft clay and laminated into a panel of wet paperclay to create a textural surface.

layer of clay in a juddering motion, to settle it into the crevices and round the grog pieces, also building up the thickness a little.

Alternatively, a soft clay slab can be placed carefully over some fragments and compressed into position with the flat of the hand, and then carefully with a roller. This method is slightly problematic as some of the fragments will come loose, but that does leave interesting cavities in the clay; using smaller particles will also remedy this.

After the tests have been fired, the colours will intensify and the fragments are a jumble on the surface. If the grog is made of porcelain and only initially fired at a low biscuit temperature, this will enable the surface to be sanded with ease as the clay will still be quite soft, so a smoother finish and a more level surface can be produced.

INLAID SURFACE COLOUR

This method, also referred to as appliqué, comprises thin layers or coils of coloured clay that are arranged on a freshly rolled-out panel of soft clay, and then compressed into the surface as applied decoration.

Using a sheet of newsprint, the pieces can be pushed into place with a plastic rib or a rolling pin. This will spread the colour out and depending how much pressure is applied, will stretch the design further.

This technique can be adapted to use on a leather-hard surface with a soft, coloured clay mixture as before, but using a transfer method. Pieces of the soft, coloured clay are smeared unevenly on to a smooth cloth with a knife or the fingertips and left to stiffen a little; however, they are not allowed to dry completely.

Slender coils of different coloured clays are arranged in a pattern on the surface of a soft sheet of clay.

When the fragments are compressed and inlaid into the surface, the colours spread out and merge slightly together.

Another coloured clay has been added to provide some more detail, and left slightly raised on the surface.

Sticky coloured clays have been smeared on a panel of cotton cloth with a knife and allowed to stiffen.

The coloured clay is transferred by applying pressure on to the back of the cotton, before it is peeled away.

At this stage the cloth can be manipulated, forcing the clay to crack slightly, but making sure the fragments are still stuck to the cloth. It is placed face down on to slightly damp clay, pressing the cloth with the flat of your hand or a roller, to ensure the coloured clay fragments are embedded into the surface, before peeling the cloth away.

Yellow clay has been smeared on to the clay surface, using the fingertips to apply a smoother area and a more gestural surface.

Additional layers of coloured clay are smeared through different stencils to create an embossed, raised design.

Another method that works well with a very soft mixture is to smear it directly on to a nearly leather-hard surface to create a background for additional colours; depending on how it is applied, it can produce a textural quality to the surface.

Commercial plastic stencils can be used to smear another layer of decoration on to the surface, using different colours to build a design, resulting in a slightly embossed surface.

Yvette Glaze and her Use of Coloured Clay

Yvette Glaze is a ceramic artist who also uses coloured clay as part of her repertoire of decorative surface techniques. Yvette has followed an interesting creative path, which has guided her passion for mark making. Her training in stage design led her to a career as a scenic artist and prop maker, and she then spent many years teaching art and ceramics in psychiatric hospitals and working with people with learning disabilities. Teaching in this field has had a profound impact on her creative work: exploring and experimenting with mixed media became intertwined, and she is drawn inextricably to the emotional response of a subject.

Yvette is fascinated by old boats and will often go to Rye and Hastings near where she lives to draw the fishing community there. She feels the boats retain a story and an emotional imprint, which can be seen and felt through the layers of the paint and rust. Her visual research is alive with colour and texture, and a testament to that emotional response:

I always begin with sketchbooks. I paint instinctively to try to capture how I feel about an image, rather than exactly how it looks. I love using multiple layers and techniques in this process. This includes acrylic paint, mono print, lino print, inks, and collage. The sketchbooks have a spontaneous quality which I love.

Yvette then moves on to clay and tries to capture the same unconstrained approach, using the clay surface like a canvas and echoing the same processes in layers as she does on paper. She has developed an elaborate visual language, and it is the surface that plays a vital role in the finished pieces. She is constantly moving on, experimenting and finding new ways of working.

Yvette will begin with the paper resist and mono print techniques to capture the beginning of the image, and then uses stencils to apply coloured clay, embossing with lino blocks to add texture. To add further depth, she draws using the sgraffito method, then applies underglazes and oxides, often adding areas of coloured or transparent glaze depending on the piece. She works with her sketchbooks around her, acting as a guide: 'They give inspiration, but I try to find a flow where I follow my instincts. All my surfaces are unique as they are captured in the moment.'

A selection of vessels by ceramic artist Yvette Glaze, on the shelves of her studio. She uses a variety of decorative techniques to create the multi-layered surfaces.

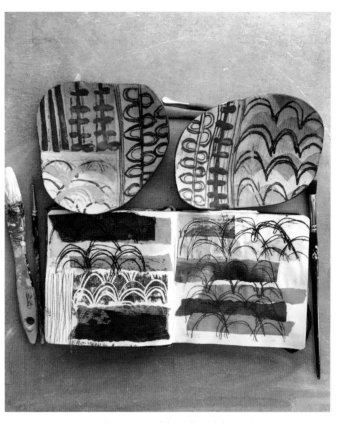

Yvette tries to capture the essence of the collaged, layered approach she achieves in her visual research, translating that spontaneity on to the clay.

Sketchbooks are integral to Yvette's creative practice. She has developed an elaborate visual language that plays a vital role in her work.

Yvette works with her sketchbooks around her, acting as a guide, giving her inspiration to develop each unique surface.

CONFETTI METHOD

This technique uses the coloured clay shavings and small peelings that are often left over from other projects, and involves compacting the fragments together to produce a confetti-like surface. Firm and even softer clay can be grated if more fragments are needed. It is advisable when collecting these scraps that they are used in a leather-hard state, which will help to fuse them together. Arrange them on a block of plaster, making sure they are grouped together in an even layer, so a dense, flat surface can be achieved.

Lightly mist the clay with water, then place a sheet of newsprint over the surface and flatten it with a mallet or a flat spatula, by tapping evenly over the surface. This has more control when initially compacting the colour together, but after it has been peeled away from the plaster a rolling pin can be used to stretch it a little more.

A more delicate panel can be made from the scraps by placing the fragments in a more linear design on the plaster, using a wooden tool or a soft brush to guide the small fragments into place. Lightly mist with water and use the same method to flatten the particles. They can also be sprinkled into a simple stencil, pressing the colour fragments into the shapes with the fingertips, smoothing the surface of the clay until it is level, and wiping away any excess of clay on the surface of the stencil. As the stencil is peeled away from the plaster, the fragments may stay in the spaces of the stencil, so just push them gently through with the fingertips to release them.

There are a few ways that these prepared fragments can be used. They can be laminated on to another sheet of soft or leather-hard clay that has been lightly misted with water. Peel the compressed colour fragments away from the plaster using a thin, firm rib or a metal kidney, and place the fragments on to the clay surface. They need to be placed face up, which was the side that had been face down on the plaster. Use a thin sheet of transparent plastic so it is easy to see what is happening, and stretch it over the surface, smoothing it out so there are no wrinkles, and use the fingertips or a soft rib to laminate them into place. The confetti clay pieces can also be embedded into a panel of wet liquid paperclay.

Let the paperclay layer settle for a while before applying the compacted fragments, so it will sit on top of the surface and not sink too far into the liquid. Alternatively, the fragments can stay on the plaster and a layer of liquid paperclay can be poured over the back of the design and while they are still stuck to the surface. In both cases they can be peeled away carefully, once they have gone solid, but are still flexible. This 'confetti' method can also be used to create a shallow vessel using a press mould. A pestle wrapped in muslin can be used to compress the colour fragments together, adding them gradually into a mould, aiming for an even distribution and thickness until the surface of the mould has been filled in; because of the method of construction, it should be allowed to dry very slowly.

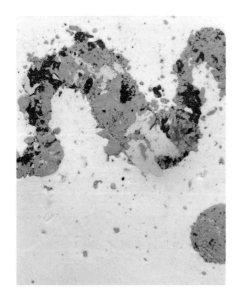

A thin, delicate layer of compressed colour can be laminated on to a leather-hard surface or applied to a freshly cast layer of liquid paperclay.

Confetti-like fragments have been arranged together on a plaster block, using a pastry cutter to define the shape.

The fragments have been pressed firmly together to create a multi-coloured panel of clay, then slightly stretched with a rolling pin.

Underglaze Colour Fragments

The confetti method will also work with the dried fragments of commercial liquid underglazes, which often accumulate inside the surface of the containers. The dried colour can be scraped out and stored separately, until there is a range of different colours to use.

As they are dry and the fragments go quite hard, they must be applied to a wet or soft surface. Crush the colour to adjust the size of the fragments, using a rolling pin over a sheet of newsprint.

Stencils can be used to contain the tiny shards into specific shapes on a block of plaster, using the same process as the coloured clay fragments. Mist lightly with water to hold them in place, then apply a layer of soft clay over the top, or liquid paperclay can be poured carefully over the surface, taking care not to dislodge the pattern.

They can also be sprinkled directly on to a panel of liquid paperclay that has been allowed to stiffen for a while, and a paper stencil can be applied on a section, to guide the spread of the fragments. Press any loose shards carefully with the tips of the fingers and push them into the surface, just enough to ensure they are embedded a little way, so they stay in place.

REVERSE INLAY PROCESS

One of the most inventive decorative techniques I have come across was developed by American ceramist Aurore Chabot, currently the Professor of Ceramic Art at the University of Arizona. She devised a method of making mosaic-like surfaces, which she refers to as the 'reverse inlay process'.

I came across her work while a student on the Summer Programme at the Banff Centre for Arts and Creativity in Canada in the late eighties. As a visiting artist, she hand-built a large structure incorporating this technique and on a demanding scale.

Her process and inspirational approach to creating such a surface has stayed with me, and over the years I have taught versions of her method to students, though on a more modest scale and improvising with materials that included incorporating coloured clay alongside painted surfaces.

What made Aurore's technique so appealing was that her construction method demanded that the image was often only revealed once the surface had been completed, and in some cases after the firing. Aurore would prepare panels of

The dried remnants of the liquid underglaze colours can be collected until there is a range of colours, ideal to use with the confetti method.

Small slivers of underglaze colour have been sprinkled on to a plaster block through a cardboard stencil, prior to covering with clay.

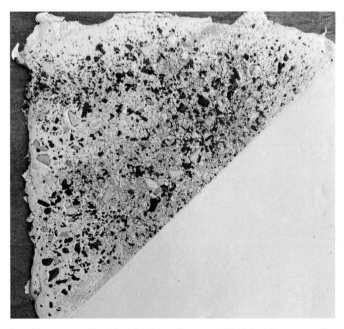

Dried fragments of liquid underglaze colours, sprinkled directly on to a soft porcelain paperclay panel, using paper to mask a section.

'Just a Snip' by American ceramist Aurore Chabot, incorporating her reverse inlay process into the surface. (PHOTO: BALFOUR WALKER)

A detail of one of Aurore Chabot's ceramic constructions 'Wormwould', with painted fragments embedded into the surface.

'Une Coupe de Gateaux', made during a demonstration by American ceramist Aurore Chabot at the Banff Centre for Arts and Creativity in Canada.

A collection of small, modelled constructed forms by Aurore Chabot, referred to as 'memory fossils', part of her reverse inlay process.

'Three Minus One' by Aurore Chabot, under construction and built upside down, allowing the reverse inlay fragments to stay together.

'Cataclysm' by Aurore Chabot, with details of her reverse inlay technique and incorporating her memory fossils. (PHOTO: BALFOUR WALKER)

leather-hard clay that she painted with elaborate and bold geometric patterns in underglaze colours. She would also make small fragments – modelled, constructed forms that she calls 'memory fossils' – also meticulously painted in different colours.

The painted slab was then 'fragmented' – that is, cut or torn into smaller sections – and placed face down quite close together on to a strong but smooth fabric; the memory fossils were incorporated into the surface treatment. This would be supported by a specially constructed 'mould' to create the form, sometimes consisting of vermiculite-filled cloth bags, panels of wood fixed at different angles with hinges, found plaster forms, or cloth-covered boards.

This inlay method was used not only on Aurore's sculptural pieces, but also on large murals in tile form. Soft clay was added gradually to the back of the roughened and moistened fragments, and was also pressed firmly in between the gaps to reveal conglomerate slabs. These became the basis for the structures, completed upside down to allow the inlaid panel to be supported during the making, as moving them at this stage would certainly risk the fragments coming apart.

Aurore's work has been inspired by her travels to Barcelona, to pay homage to the ceramic-laden concrete architecture of Antonio Gaudí, and to Mexico, where she could indulge her fascination with rituals, shrines and temples associated with the Mexican and Spanish celebration of the 'Day of the Dead', where individual artistry of creating elaborate tombs is honoured and practised. More recently, a sabbatical research trip led her to numerous museum collections, where she explored and documented the rich and diverse qualities of Tibetan Buddhist Art and iconography that also honours rituals of death, which she has incorporated into her art.

Aurore talks about her approach to her work:

I am guided by the seemingly discordant sensibilities of geometric and organic systems to create hybrid forms with negative spaces that pass through and into the sculptures. The pieces are simple, yet contain compositional elements in complex arrangements, including layers of tile and fossil-like fragments, carved and distressed surfaces, bright colours against raw, blackish metallic stains, and the residue of personal dream symbols. Across my life as an artist I have striven to bring dynamic energy to my art in which layers of 'memory fossils' embedded in biomorphic and architectonic compositions serve as a metaphor for traveling through a lifetime of time, experience and consciousness.

Mosaic Fragments

A smaller and more modest version of Aurore's reverse inlay technique uses smaller fragments, made from painted, printed or coloured clay panels, which are combined together with liquid porcelain paperclay and can work with a combination of different clays. The patterned sheets of clay can be cut into abstract pieces, precise shapes, or torn into sections and then re-arranged together.

Once the decisions have been made about their positioning, the pieces are turned over, so they are face down on to a plaster block and the liquid paperclay is trailed carefully into the gaps between the fragments to join them together. The paperclay liquid can be diluted to adjust the consistency if it is proving too thick to inlay evenly between the sections, but this can also create interesting recesses into the design – it's just a matter of preference.

Take care as the gaps are filled as the pieces may shift, but if the first layer is allowed to set a little, it will secure them into place and then an additional layer of paperclay can be smeared over the back of the panel to reinforce it. As it dries,

the clay will sink down and the edges of the fragments may become visible; extra paperclay can be added if required. The surface on the back can be smoothed over with a rib to help compress the fragments and the paperclay together. Once the clay has become firm the panel can be peeled away from the plaster block.

To add another element to the design, an engraved stamp can be pressed into the appliquéd surface, creating an embossed surface to the mosaic pieces.

Underglaze colour or oxide can be applied into the recesses or gaps between the fragments after they have been biscuit fired to highlight any detail.

The surface can also be polished with wet-and-dry sandpaper – keep dipping the biscuit-fired panels into a bowl of water and wetting the abrasive paper regularly during the sanding process; this will create a smooth, pebble-like finish. It can also erode any seepage from the paperclay inlay around the tile fragments that has attached itself to the coloured surface.

After the final firing the colours will change, and porcelain especially will give a vibrancy to the finished surface.

A panel of decorated clay, using the printed slip transfer technique can be used to create mosaic fragments for the reverse inlay method.

A piece of printed clay has been torn into pieces, creating mosaic-style fragments in preparation for the reverse inlay method.

A panel of different inlaid coloured clays has been cut into more precise sections, ready to be laid out face down on to a plaster block.

All the edges that have been trimmed off the coloured clay panels have not been wasted, as they can be used to create another panel.

Liquid porcelain paperclay is trailed carefully between the clay pieces so as not to dislodge any, and securing them into place.

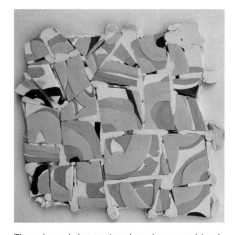

The coloured clay sections have been combined together, making a feature of the indentations and gaps left, when trailing the paperclay slip.

To add further detail, a carved biscuit stamp has been used to emboss a repetitive leaf pattern over the surface while it is still soft.

To highlight the detail, oxides or underglaze colour are painted into the crevices, helping to emphasize the torn edges.

After their final firing, the inlaid colours have intensified and the embossed detail highlights the abstract fragments in the design.

The leftover pieces have been combined, and the textural qualities of the different clays used have become more defined.

CHAPTER 7

MIXED MEDIA

Many potters are taking on a more experimental approach to their creative practice and incorporating other materials into their work at different stages of the making. Challenging the perceptions of how clay could be used has intrigued many makers. Ceramics is arguably amongst the few media to have endured the test of time. Many potters are still inspired by this ancient craft and its traditions, which has remained its strength, but have advanced the boundaries of what ceramics can be, embracing the sheer versatility of this medium.

ADDITIONS TO THE CLAY BODY

Adding other materials can present a remarkable range of dynamic marks and textures to a ceramic surface, highlighting the importance of experimenting with different ingredients. This can include hard additions such as glass frit, crushed marble, rust, or materials such as vermiculite, a naturally occurring mineral, and perlite, which is made of expanded volcanic glass – both are used in plant propagation. There is also an array of combustible and organic matter to explore, such as

A Marotte head made by animator Jo Lawrence, using layers of fibreglass, porcelain paperclay and printed collage.

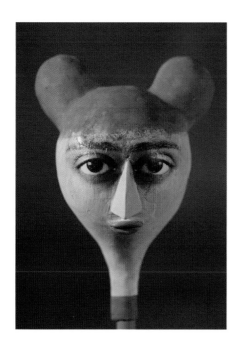

◀ 'Arithmetic', by American ceramic artist Mitch Lyons, who devised a way to create archival prints on fabric with clay. (PHOTO: MEREDITH WAKEFIELD)

WHAT YOU WILL NEED

Collecting materials that can be incorporated into ceramic experiments can develop into a long-term project, and when working in mixed media, having access to a range of organic or man-made items will enable a wider range of tests.

Equipment
- Plaster blocks
- Rolling pin
- Rolling-out cloth or board
- Wooden battens
- Potter's craft knife or a Kiridashi knife
- Mallet
- Plaster cottles
- Rusted metal sheet

Materials
- Two or more different clay bodies
- Liquid porcelain paperclay
- Fibreglass – finishing tissue
- Brushes
- Plastic ribs
- Ceramic stains or oxides
- Newsprint or cotton cloth
- Mixed-media materials – combustible, organic and hard additions
- Metal leaf and size

A selection of some of the many combustible materials and hard additions that can be explored and embedded into soft clay to create embossed and textured surfaces. 'Swarf' describes the shavings that are a result of machining metal, and 'scale' is the by-product of the forging process. These were collected from the blacksmith's workshop next to the author's studio. From left to right:

1. Metal swarf
2. Lentils
3. Hundreds and thousands
4. Crushed coffee beans
5. Metal scale
6. Steel wool
7. Seaweed
8. Crushed walnut
9. Rice
10. Copper strands
11. Crushed beach brick
12. Glass frit
13. Dried plant husks and seeds

sawdust, straw, rice, seeds, coffee grains, and even hundreds and thousands, the tiny sugar beads used for decorating cakes.

Wild clay and found granular materials can be embedded into the clay, but can prove to be a challenge, especially if there are any shells or calcium-bearing rock such as limestone present. When fired, the calcined material becomes unstable and slowly reacts to moisture in the atmosphere, converting into quicklime, and the surface will start to disintegrate. Some makers will wash and pre-fire all found materials, while others, aware of the risks, will throw caution to the wind and embrace the possibilities their experiments can offer.

To have more control over the process of hard additions, coloured grog can be added to the surface. This can be made by firing fragments of stained clay to around 900°C (1652°F) and crushing them to the size required. Embedding unfired stained fragments will also work, but they will soften and may start to blend into the base clay rather than appearing as distinct particles – but both methods are worth exploring. More details about how to mix coloured clay and make coloured grog can be found in Chapter 6.

Combining metal and clay can yield dramatic results, but as the clay dries and starts to shrink, this will lead to some movement and possible stress fractures around the metal inclusions – yet this is the reason why some makers find it so appealing. Applications of glaze can often help to support any fragile sections and fuse them back into the surface. Other precautions to help minimize cracking include inserting the metal fragments at the leather-hard stage, or enlarging the gaps around the metal to allow for shrinkage.

Metal will melt at different temperatures, but will also become brittle if fired too high, so adjusting the firing temperatures to retain the quality of the metal is recommended. If strength is required, potters will favour nichrome wire as it will withstand high temperatures and will not change in structure. Steel dressmaking pins, tacks and staples can be inserted into the surface to create spiky, thorny surfaces. Steel will start to disintegrate from around 1200°C (2192°F), so low or mid-range temperatures would help preserve the quality of the metal.

Glass is another material that has always been popular with makers and can add a sparkly detail to a surface. Glass will start

A collection of test tiles with different combustible materials embedded into the surface of soft clay tiles and left to dry.

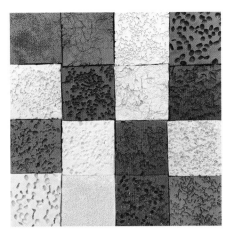

The test tiles after biscuit firing, which has burnt away all the combustible materials and left an array of different cavities.

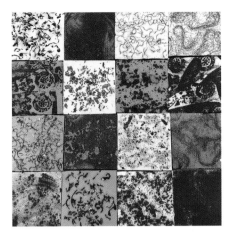

Metal additions applied into the surface of the clay have survived the firing and left bold, dark and textural surfaces.

to soften at around 760°C (1400°F), but this will depend on the type of glass and the size of the fragments. Fragments and chips of found glass can be used, but it can also be bought in various forms such as frit, which resembles sugar grains, stringers, rods of glass and confetti, which are paper-thin shards of glass. All are available in many colours and are used for applications such as glass fusing, glass slumping and glass casting. Glass will, however, tolerate a higher temperature if it is embedded into the clay surface or confined to a space to prevent it from spilling out. If the quality of water trickling over the surface is desired, be mindful of the risk of it running on to the kiln shelf, so fire that type of test on a bed of sand as a precaution.

To try out the varied materials that are on offer, it is worth making a series of test tiles. Try using a white stoneware body and a contrasting body – a terracotta crank, for example. A selection of hard materials and combustible ingredients can be embedded into soft clay panels with a rolling pin, using a sheet of newsprint or a cotton cloth to protect the surface. This can be done by placing the clay panel face down over the fragments, or sprinkling the material on to the soft clay.

Lay out the tiles on a firm surface, with a sheet of newspaper over the top. I used several sheets of cement board and stacked them together to keep them flat, allowing them to dry evenly. After the work has been biscuit fired, the combustible materials will have burned away completely, leaving cavities in the surface.

Metal inclusions will react quite differently and will leave bold markings with textural deposits. Wire wool, iron powder, copper scourer strands, metal scale and metal swarf are all worth exploring.

FIBREGLASS

Fibreglass is a reinforced woven material, and the strands are laid across each other and held together with a binding substance. Traditionally combined with a resin to form an extremely strong and durable composite, it is used in several applications and industries. It has proved to be beneficial to potters, and is used to reinforce joints and corners when hand building. It can be used independently with layers of liquid clay to create a very thin fabric, making constructions or components to embellish a surface – when fired, the fibreglass will melt and fuse into the clay.

This material has proved very popular with my students as it can produce wafer-thin fragments that have the quality of crumbled paper, which can be difficult to recreate in clay. We use a fibreglass surfacing tissue, sometimes referred to as 'surfacing veil', as this smoother, more refined version yields the best result for creating the delicate surfaces the students want to achieve. This is also safer to handle as the surface of the tissue is sealed, but if experimenting with a more substantial sheet or the loose fragments, these may irritate the skin, so wear gloves for protection.

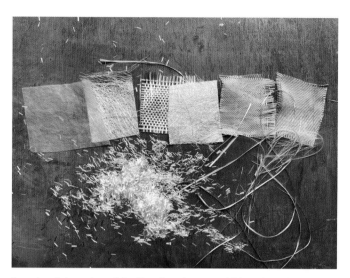

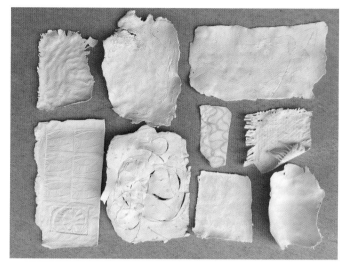

Samples of the variety of the fibreglass sheets available, including strands and threads that can be used in ceramic projects.

Different grades of fibreglass have been painted with liquid paperclay, embossed with a stamp, and colour applied between layers.

Fibreglass comes in a variety of different woven surfaces and different weights that resemble fabric, long individual strands or chopped fragments: these can all be combined with clay.

To create the surface, the fibreglass is coated on both sides with liquid porcelain paperclay, which creates a strong bond but will still retain its translucency. The slip is painted over a single layer of the tissue, using a plaster block as support. Depending on the structure or components, additional sheets can be added and laminated together with additional coats of the paperclay slip. Colour can be applied at this stage, on the final surface, or even between the layers. Once the clay has lost its shine, but is still flexible, the slip-coated tissue can be peeled away from the plaster, cut up, folded and manipulated into repetitive shapes or curved structures. The smaller components can be added to a hand-built form, which acts as a support. The liquid paperclay can be used as a slurry to join any edges together and fix multiple fragments into place.

When creating such fragile structures, it is safer to fire straight to a stoneware temperature, around 1200°C (2192°F)–1260°C (2300°F). The fibre will start to melt at around 1190°C (2174°F) and will fuse with the clay, but will retain its glassy quality. Some forms can be supported with ceramic fibre to stop them slumping, and if that is the case, glaze cannot be used. Ceramic fibre is immune to thermal shock and is used in the construction of raku kilns. It is important that gloves and a mask are used when handling this material as it will irritate the skin and the fibres should not be inhaled. Three makers I have worked with during my studio workshops were beguiled by the properties that fibreglass could offer, which resulted in their creating structures and components with such diverse imagery. Their experiments illustrate how inventive this material can be, and at times, challenging.

Jo Lawrence, Filmmaker in Mixed Media

Jo Lawrence is an animation director and maker, working in London. Her mixed-media films have been broadcast and screened widely at international film festivals. As a filmmaker, she usually works solely with animation, puppetry and photography. She wanted to create a series of porcelain heads for an exhibition entitled 'New Doggerland', and wanted to experiment with alternative methods of making. Her fascination with paper and collage led her to explore the delights of fibreglass, as she wanted to emulate some of those qualities she could achieve in her filmmaking.

The inspiration came from the practice of carrying Marottes, heads on sticks with articulated mouths, which originated in mediaeval England, where jesters carried small replicas of themselves. They were often carried during processions and were used to disseminate news and ideas through song. Jo tells the story behind the finished pieces: 'I re-imagined rejected rubbish as precious archaeological finds of the Anthropocene and the imagined formation of a New Doggerland, made from accumulated waste washed up in the North Sea, giving rise to a future culture inspired by the visual overload of plastic detritus.'

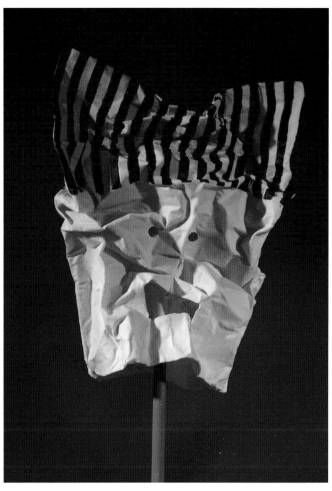

Making the Marottes

Jo applied generous layers of porcelain slip on to fibreglass sheets. Each layer of glass fibre was sandwiched together by applying another layer of porcelain slip. The resulting material was allowed to dry just a little under a plastic sheet, before crumpling and folding it into the heads. She recalls:

About six layers seemed to be the minimum, but if I were to repeat these experiments, I would aim for about eight layers of glass fibre as my previous experiments were too fragile, particularly at the edges. I treated the layered sheets as if they were a single sheet of paper, crumpling it, then shaping it into the required form. Some of the hollow structures needed support during the making, so I used a crumpled ball of newspaper as a support. Underglaze colours were painted on before firing and a transparent glaze was applied in selected areas. I used Laser Tran decals on some of the heads post firing to add photographic detail. I would have preferred to use ceramic transfer techniques, but I found the idea of controlling the colour relationships too problematical when applied at different stages of the firing process.

Jo Lawrence chose to use fibreglass as she wanted to emulate crumpled paper and to reflect her work as an animator. (PHOTO: SIMON TAYLOR)

Jo Lawrence's collection of ceramic Marottes, made with fibreglass and paperclay sheets, with photographic detail applied post firing. (PHOTO: SIMON TAYLOR)

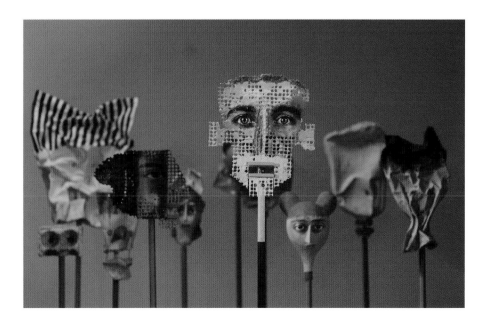

Nadine Bell and her Marine-Inspired Pieces

Nadine's passion for clay ran alongside her career as a massage therapist, but a move back to her native country enabled her to set up her studio in rural France, where she had more time and space to explore her ideas using different materials, and to experiment with firing techniques. She explains:

> I worked for twenty years as a masseuse, using my hands to help people explore the links between bodies, minds and individual wellbeing. This enabled me to neatly transition into expressing myself through ceramics, and allowing me to discover wonderful similarities when exploring the joy and creativity of clay with its memory and texture.

Nadine wanted to investigate the relationship between fragility and permanence, and looked to the sea for her inspiration. She chose a simple aquatic animal that has been around for more than 543 million years, and 5,500 species are known to exist. Sea sponges display every colour imaginable with delicate, glass-like structures, and Nadine took on the challenge to emulate these ancient creatures, using liquid clay and fibreglass tissue,

which she chose for its delicacy, fine texture and ethereal finish. She says: 'It has the potential for sculptural exploration, but combining organic subtlety.'

Making the Marine Structures

Nadine starts by hand building an enclosed form in porcelain paperclay to serve as a base for her marine-inspired pieces. She then paints two layers of paperclay slip on to a double layer of fibreglass tissue, which is supported on a block of plaster. While the surface is still tacky, a woven nylon mesh is placed carefully over the surface and a layer of cobalt oxide or powdered commercial stain is sifted on the mesh using a tea strainer to create a speckled layer; then the mesh is peeled away to reveal a ripple pattern. The tissue is cut into 3cm or 4cm strips and then into small or larger squares depending on the scale of component she wants. These are carefully scrunched individually into the required shape, taking care not to damage the decorated surface. The fragments are attached very closely together on to the porcelain structure, using the paperclay slip, gradually assembling an undulating fragile surface.

She is drawn to the concept of the traditional Japanese aesthetics wabi-sabi, and is inspired by the thought of finding beauty in every aspect of imperfection in nature, combined with her love for the unknown. She explains: 'This philosophy nurtures all that is authentic by acknowledging three simple realities: nothing lasts, nothing is finished, nothing is perfect.'

Isis Dove-Edwin and her Exploration of Fibreglass

Isis Dove-Edwin had her first contact with clay as a medical student, seeking a creative outlet. Getting back to clay during a career break, she explored surface and shape in functional forms. Although she experimented with non-functional work, she realized that to take this further, and push the critical boundaries of her practice, she needed an immersive, structured environment, and so enrolled in the BA Ceramic Design programme at Central St Martins, in London. More recently, her work has developed to explore and document historical and contemporary social themes primarily relating to the Black African diaspora. It is heavily research based, often bringing to light marginalized or overlooked narratives. She started an MA in Ceramics and Glass at the Royal College of Art in September 2021.

Nadine Bell's fascination with ancient sea sponges prompted an exploration into creating a delicate surface using fibreglass tissue.

Isis Dove-Edwin created wafer-thin vessels that were inspired by a forlorn bandstand and the demise of communal entertainment in local parks.

Isis is attracted to the infinite potential of clay to hold memory, and express different ideas through materiality, process and form. She is fascinated by the power of ceramics to provide documentation of everyday life, events and ideas, which can be shared in their time, through gift, exchange or exhibition, as well as into the future as inherited, heritage objects or found archaeological objects.

Making the Vessels

These fibreglass pieces were part of Isis exploring and experimenting with different materials prior to her BA, and they were inspired by a forlorn bandstand, which made her think about the decline in outdoor communal entertainment in local parks. Fibreglass sheets were cut to size, painted with porcelain paperclay slip, and decorated with bold stripes of underglaze colour. Before the sheets were dry, they were wrapped around a cylindrical form. Once placed on a kiln shelf, a blanket of ceramic fibre was inserted into the forms to help support the shape, but there were gaps into which the porcelain could melt and wrinkle, to give a sense of wear and neglect. The forms were not glazed, and were fired once to 1220°C (2228°F), after which the ceramic fibre was carefully removed.

INCORPORATING OTHER MATERIALS

Mixed media has been integrated into my practice over the years, and I have often included other materials into my work as a way of keeping alive an experimental environment to stretch my ideas.

I use the found materials as a vehicle for my research and the development of concepts, and will select and incorporate some of the experiments into the work, but will also use found ceramic fragments to decorate and refire. In some of my experiments, I used reclaimed ceramic roof tiles as background, refiring them with dry glazes, applying underglaze colour or packing them into a saggar firing.

I have used sea-weathered brick fragments and refired them, applying underglaze colour, using wax-resist techniques. Casting fragments using glass frit in plaster moulds have also gone

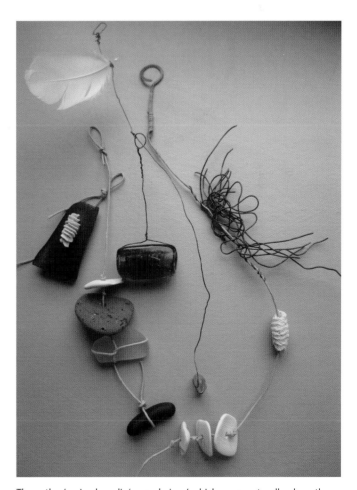

The author's mixed-media 'meanderings', which represent walks along the beach, her love of beachcombing, and discovering little gems.

One of the author's mixed-media experiments, using vintage roof tiles, refired with ceramic pigments and embellished with a structure cast in glass frit.

A mixed-media construction by the author, incorporating a fragment of brick, weathered by the sea and printed with underglaze colour.

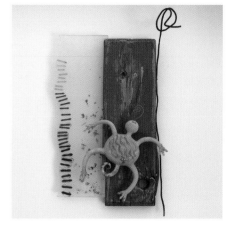

A ceramic turtle by the author, mounted on distressed wood, with twisted steel and a sheet of glass, fused with fragments of glass confetti and stringers.

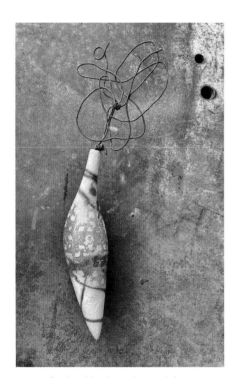

Saggar-fired pod by the author, with fragments of copper leaf, and a flattened steel wire bundle, used to bind lengths of steel delivered to the forge.

Fragments of gold leaf that are left over on the paper backings are known as scewings, and can prove to be very useful to decorate a surface.

into the mix. Some experiments include incorporating panels of glass into a piece, fused with slivers of coloured glass.

Many makers have used silver, gold and copper leaf or foil to enhance a piece post firing – a metallic glimmer can enrich a surface and make all the difference. It can be applied over a glaze or on an unglazed surface, applied in panels so a smooth even surface can be achieved, or just in sections, in a pattern, or distressed with a stiff brush to give a weathered appearance. All metals are available as loose leaves or as transfer leaves backed with a white paper, which is the best option as it is much easier to control and apply to a ceramic surface.

A layer of traditional size needs to be used as part of the application, and there are acrylic versions that are adhesives with an extended open time for bonding metal leaf and foils to a variety of surfaces. The 'open time' relates to the time it can be worked on before the size dries completely, which varies from one to two hours, and up to twenty-four hours. Acrylic yacht varnish is a good alternative, and I use this to print on to the ceramic surface using sponge stamps to create a pattern where the metallic foil will be applied. The effect I like when using gold foil, for example, is the abstracted fragments often left over that are still attached to the paper and known as scewings: these have a wonderful quality about them.

The coating of size is left to go tacky to the touch, and the foil is then applied to the surface and smoothed into place with the fingertips; the backing paper is then peeled away. Spaces can be left for effect, or more sections of foil can be added to fill in the gaps. The foil can be burnished with a soft cloth, and there is the option to seal the metallic surface with a matt acrylic varnish.

Found materials will often provide a vital element, and makers choose to incorporate fragments from their collections into their work as additions post-firing, as they are an important contribution to the finished pieces.

Elaine Bolt and her Use of Found Objects

Found objects are hugely meaningful to Elaine, and she says: 'Found objects seem to strongly embody a place and a time, where and when they were found, but also the mystery of where they might have been, and how long they have been "lost" in nature.'

Found fragments are a crucial element to Elaine Bolt's work, where the boundaries between made and found are blurred. (PHOTO: YESHEN VENEMA)

The meticulous structure of the forms she collects pulls her in and makes her want to look more and more closely. She is also drawn to objects that have weathered over time, and have often taken on new characteristics from their environment, furnishing them with a patina or a fascinating texture. Elaine collects various types of found objects and natural materials both from the shoreline and increasingly from the local landscape of the South Downs in Sussex, which includes fragments such as twigs, alder cones, lichen, thorns and seeds. These must be sourced at certain times of the year, and she uses her regular walks on the Downs to collect from her favourite places. These materials often need to be stored up to a year or more, to ensure they are properly dried before use.

Found materials are incorporated into her mixed-media constructions, embedded into the composition with small

Found materials are incorporated into Elaine Bolt's mixed-media constructions, embedded with small abstract porcelain pieces. (PHOTO: ALUN CALLENDER)

Elaine's porcelain 'Woodland Vessels', using twigs and porcelain fragments that emerge from the rims. (PHOTO: ALUN CALLENDER)

PAPERCLAY

Paper pulp added to clay will extend its creative possibilities. It is extremely versatile, warp free and light after firing. The opportunity to be experimental allows the maker to be more of an artist and less of a technician. The joys of working with such an adaptable material allows greater flexibility to be able to incorporate other materials. It is an ideal medium in liquid form, to use in the various printing methods using a plaster block and it can also produce delicate detailed casts of plant fragments.

Lace, crochet or textured fabric can be dipped in paperclay slip, then carefully hung up, preventing the fragments from folding over. Textured paper and leaves, for example, can just be coated on one side to replicate every detail. Twisted bundles of cotton wool can be dipped and applied immediately to a clay surface to create clusters of organic-type cavities over the surface. Fragments of seaweed, fish bones or seed pods can be coated carefully with several layers so as not to flood the detail.

The cast fragments can be applied to another sheet of clay or to a structure as embellishments, using liquid clay as slurry to attach them to the surface. This can be done when the pieces are bone dry or attached when very wet. The paperclay can

abstract hand-made porcelain pieces. The wall pieces she creates are a form of collage, where the boundaries between the made and the found are blurred. Elaine's porcelain 'Woodland Vessels' have twigs embedded into and emerging from their rims. Materials such as acorn cups and lichen are also attached, along with porcelain pieces as if they are growing from the piece itself. Recently, Elaine has been using natural materials directly in her making process, adding seeds and lichen to the surface of a pot and painting slip over them. When they burn away in the kiln, they create a natural random pattern on the surface.

Elaine has a shelf where many of her most treasured found objects are placed, along with bundles of willow twigs and other items that she has collected. She also has drawers where she stores her found materials, sorted into wood, metals, plastics and organic matter. She also keeps the small porcelain pieces she has made in boxes, sorting them by shape, size and colour. She rarely makes these with a specific goal in mind, but keeps them and uses them as if they were found objects with the same status.

Porcelain paperclay casts of the Chinese lantern plant made by the author have been adorned with laser-cut leaf shapes in brass.

also be stained with oxides and commercial stains, or washes of colour can be applied when they are dry, but will work very well as pure white, enhancing their delicate nature.

All organic matter and natural fibres will burn away in the firing, but be careful not to use any nylon or plastic as this will create toxic fumes and may leave a residue as they melt.

Linear drawings of paperclay can be applied on to plaster with a slip trailer freehand, or the designs can be drawn in pencil, directly on to the plaster block which is used as a guide.

Once the initial outline is trailed, extra layers will need to be applied to link the elements of pattern together and make it robust enough to come away from the plaster in one piece. If the aim is to create very fine lines, a trailer with small nozzles will clog up quite easily due to the fibrous nature of the paperclay. They will have to be unblocked using a dressmaker's pin at regular intervals – it's a bit fiddly but it will work. Alternatively aim for trailers with a more generous tip. The completed fragments tend to be quite fragile so they need to be leather hard

Accurate casts of leaves can be made when the porcelain paperclay is applied to one side of the leaf; after firing, all the delicate detail is revealed.

Plant forms can be cast if carefully coated in layers of porcelain paperclay, resulting in sculptural plant structures.

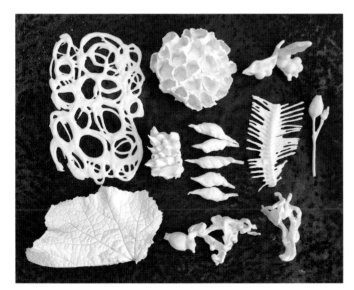

A collection of different objects that have been cast into porcelain paperclay fragments, which can be used to embellish a surface.

Ceramic stains or oxides can be mixed into the paperclay to create colourful casts, creating vibrant results.

Even the most delicate plant forms, such as this wreath of straw and dried grasses, can be rendered in paperclay if care is taken to paint on the layers.

Drawing a design on to the plaster block first can prove helpful and can act as a guide when slip trailing with paperclay.

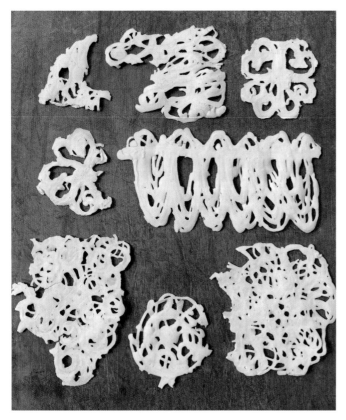

After carefully peeling away the slip-trailed fragments from the plaster, they can be fired or applied to a clay surface as laminated pieces.

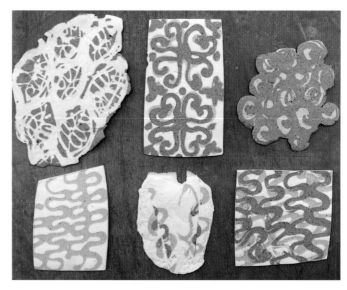

More linear, trailed designs can be held together by applying a contrasting layer of coloured porcelain to create a panel.

before attempting to remove them from the plaster: using a thin plastic rib will help with the peeling process, and this will also depend on how many layers have been applied. These can be fired independently or laminated on to a surface, using the liquid paperclay slip to fix them into place.

If single outlines are required, the trailed fragments can be backed with a thin layer of the paperclay slip, in a contrasting colour to create a panel. The panels can also be cut up and rearranged to abstract the design.

RUST PRINTING

Rust printing is a technique that is often explored by printmakers and textile artists who are especially fascinated by creating patterns with natural processes and accidental effects. This involves sandwiching layers of paper or fabric soaked in a solution of water and vinegar between sheets of ferrous metal fragments to absorb the rusty surfaces. Prints or casts can be taken from sheets of rusted metal using liquid paperclay or casting slip, and the iron oxide content in the metal will ensure a permanent colour transfer. There is an abundance of rusty metal available around my studio as there is a forge on the same site, so I will often select and forage for rusty gems as inspiration. Experimenting with a rusty surface was a natural progression, and the textural quality of weathered metal provides a tantalizing surface to try.

For my tests I poured the liquid paperclay directly on to the metal surface and just allowed it to pool. I also used cottle rings made of plaster, to help retain the slip and create more depth to the cast. If poured carefully they will stay without being fixed into place.

Underglaze colour or oxides can be painted, printed or slip trailed on to the metal before casting to provide another layer of decoration.

The paperclay slip can be poured straight on to the metal surface or into cottle rings made of plaster to contain the slip.

This experimental approach to casting, using sheets of rusted metal to create the marks, is reminiscent of the techniques used by textile artists.

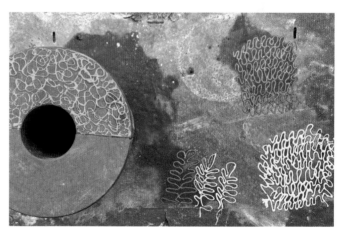

Slip-trailed underglaze colour has been applied to a sheet of rusted metal before the paperclay, to add some detail.

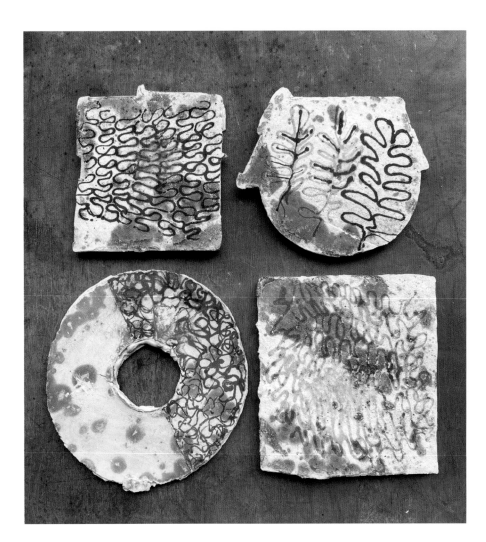

The experimental rust prints have provided the opportunity to create distinctive marks and colours from sheets of rusted metal.

Once the slip has been applied to the surface, the panels will need to dry until they are leather hard, before attempting to peel them away from the surface. This will take longer than usual as the metal surface is not porous. To speed the drying process, the panel can be very carefully heated from underneath with a heat gun. The metal panel can be propped up with kiln props in preparation before casting takes place.

Nadire Gökman and her Approach to Rust Printing

Nadire Gökmen is a London-based artist who predominantly works in ceramics; her process-led practice is motivated by the material traces that appear in a man-made environment. Nadire looked at the process of rust printing, and has taken it to a more sophisticated level: 'A desire to capture these traces,

rather than mimic them.' So in her final year of university, she developed a slip-casting process, allowing the rusted surface of steel to be directly transferred on to clay. She goes on to explain: 'The urban landscape is simultaneously dotted with traces of our presence in, and separation from nature, from orange hues that envelop steel exteriors to the rusted silhouettes of absent objects.' Initially documenting her textural surroundings through photography, Nadire wanted to capture something more physical.

Nadire starts to record her 'primary traces', as she calls them, by attaching sheets of steel to the ground outside where they are left to collect the marks accumulated through human movement and natural weathering. Nadire attached sheets of steel to surfaces chosen for their material qualities and quiet compositions – the meeting of a manhole cover with adjacent concrete,

London-based artist Nadire Gökmen has researched and developed her own approach to rust printing, creating sophisticated 'Traces'.

Nadire attaches the metal panels to locations outside, leaving them to collect marks made by human intervention or weathered by the elements.

Nadire is able to produce, through her casting process, a range of tones and colours and nuances of detail in the surface.

Nadire captures the textural qualities of a location, placing a finished piece, which has been wood fired, back to where it was slip cast.

or the mortared lines between laid bricks, for example. She explains how she develops the patinas she will cast: 'Varying rusts are produced when formed under different conditions. A sheet of steel trapped beneath another material could produce a black rust as the steel is starved of oxygen. Whereas a sheet of steel left submerged in water will produce a yellow rust.'

Nadire slip casts directly from a plaster mould placed on the rusted steel surface. The forms are then high fired, trapping the ephemeral patina of rust as a permanent trace on the clay body. The variety of iron oxides present on the steel produces an array of reds, browns, purples, pinks and blacks on the ceramic surface.

She says: 'My work elevates and makes a spectacle of the otherwise unnoticed marks captured beneath us. Predominantly hung on the wall, each form can be consistently produced, yet their surface is always unique.'

PRINTING WITH CLAY ON A FABRIC SUBSTRATE

This inventive and unique method of printing with clay was developed by the American artist Mitch Lyons. He was able to produce sophisticated and complex surfaces, combining gestural marks with experimental transfer techniques with just a clay slip, pigment and water. This technique requires layers of china clay slip mixed with pigments and applied to a panel of clay, which serves as a printing plate known as a Matrix. The image is transferred to a fabric substrate that is non-absorbent, creating an archival print that is permanent and no firing is required.

After several years of researching the most effective substrate to use, Mitch discovered a fabric called Pellon, a non-woven material often referred to as interfacing which is used in the clothing industry, but eventually opted for another fabric called Reemay which is acid-free and 100 per cent polyester. It is a strong inert material used for preservation and conservation methods. It retains its physical properties when wet and is stable during humidity change and is also used in the filtering industry. As it is manufactured with an electromagnetic surface, it allows the water to pass through, but traps the clay into the surface. Mitch also printed on sandpaper, using a fine or extra fine grade which can hold the clay because of the texture and does not require the misting with water which is essential with the Reemay fabric.

Only pure pigments, in powder or liquid form, produce the best results with this clay printing technique, and ceramic stains can be used in combination with artist's pigments. These need to be added to the slip in their raw state, as it is important to avoid any colour that contains drying agents, because this will prevent the slips from staying wet and will not release the clay slips during the printing process. The slip mixture for this technique comprises equal amounts of china clay and water. Also known as 'kaolin', this purest natural white clay is the essential ingredient for making porcelain, and is used in the production of paper. This is the perfect material to use because when pigments are added, it gives the slip a brilliant, luminous colour.

'Checkerboard', an expressive print by American artist Mitch Lyons, who developed an inventive way to print with clay. (PHOTO: MEREDITH WAKEFIELD)

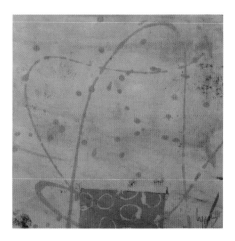

'Yellow Joy', a dynamic print by American artist Mitch Lyons, who built up layers of china clay slips with pure pigments, to create archival prints. (PHOTO: MEREDITH WAKEFIELD)

There is a wide selection of artist's pigments available: they are very strong, intense colours, so all you need are just a few spoonfuls added to the slip.

'Forgotten Feather' by Mitch Lyons, who has used a real feather to emboss into the surface of a clay block with layers of coloured slip to create a painterly print. (PHOTO: MEREDITH WAKEFIELD)

Printing with clay is very different from any other monoprint method. As the print is pulled, a thin layer of clay is transferred to the substrate; this type of printing process usually generates only one defined print and possibly a second, softer image, known as a ghost. In this case, however, there are enough layers of coloured slip left on the matrix for additional monoprints and each print will be different as the various slip layers are revealed. If the clay printing block is kept damp by being wrapped well in plastic when being stored, additional prints can still be taken from the layers left on the matrix.

Preparing the Matrix

In established printmaking methods, the matrix can be made of wood, metal, plastic or stone. This technique requires a shallow box filled with a stoneware clay body, which has a slightly gritty texture. It is important that it has an open and porous body so it will not warp, wets more evenly, and will ensure good printing results.

WHAT YOU WILL NEED

Materials for the Matrix
- Plywood panel ½in (1.27cm) thick
- Suggested sizes:
- A4: 8.3 × 11.7in (21 × 29.7cm)
- A3: 11.7 × 16.5in (42 × 29.7cm)
- Square-edge batten strips
- Wood glue/panel pins
- Clamps
- Heavy-duty plastic sheet
- Staplegun

Materials for Printing
- Newsprint
- Clay – any stoneware or mid-range clay body
- China clay
- Ceramic stains
- Artist's pigments – liquid or powder
- Reemay substrate – polyester fabric
- Dry wall or plasterboard tape
- Brushes and sponges
- Plastic rib
- Fine mist spray
- Dual hardwood roller
- Textures for embossing
- Stencils

Building the Matrix

Step 1: To create the matrix, the clay block needs to be encased in a shallow wooden tray to ensure it can be kept damp and the clay panel is supported during the printing procedure. Glue or tack some square-edge timber battens to the edges of a plywood panel to create a frame.

Step 2: Line the tray with a sheet of heavy-duty plastic and use a staple gun to secure it into place, as this will prevent the clay from drying out. Prepare a block of clay and slice it into thick, even panels with a harp or wire. Lay them into the box very close together and use a mallet to flatten them out, filling any gaps with extra clay.

Step 3: Use a length of wooden battening or a straight edge and scrape it evenly across the panel to remove any excess clay. Hold it at a slight angle and run it along the edge of the frame to avoid denting the surface. Do this in both directions to achieve an even level across the surface.

Allow the clay to get to the leather-hard stage before applying any slip. The clay needs to be firm, but still flexible enough to press textures into the surface.

To create a smooth, viscous slip mixture, add the china clay in handfuls with a few spoonfuls of pigment to a measure of water, allowing it to be absorbed, before mixing thoroughly. Aim for a thick consistency as this will guarantee a better print; however, the thickness of the slip and the intensity of colour can be adjusted by adding more china clay or more pigment.

Wooden trays are ready to fill with clay, using plastic to line the box, and a roller and newsprint to inlay the printed surface using a china clay slip.

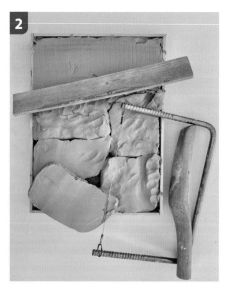

Thick slices of stoneware clay are sandwiched together to fill the tray and form a consistent layer over the whole surface.

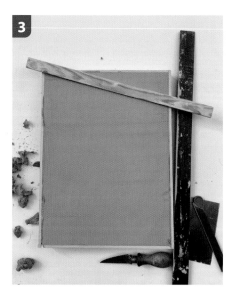

A straight-edge or wooden batten is pulled across the clay at an angle, to even out the surface, so it is level with the edges of the tray.

Applying Colour to the Matrix, Stage 1

Slip can now be applied to the clay surface, and this process can comprise many layers, using a range of colours applied in different ways, building up a complex and sophisticated surface. A variety of artist's pigments are mixed into the china-clay slip and can be applied over the clay surface, overlapping the colours to create texture and patterns using the transfer technique, stencils and found fragments.

Step 1: The whole area can be painted with a couple of coats of the first colour using a soft, flat brush, or try two blocks of flat colour, making sure each coat is allowed to lose its sheen before applying the next.

Step 2: After each new application of colour, it is important to place a clean sheet of newsprint over the matrix and use a wooden pony roller to compress the surface and inlay the slip. Different layers can be applied to the matrix using the paper transfer technique, which involves painting layers of china-clay slip on to sheets of newsprint.

Step 3: The slipped paper can be supported on a plaster block to help absorb the moisture and allow the slip on the paper to lose its sheen. These sheets can be cut or torn into sections to use in different ways as the image is built up. If at any stage they start to dry out, apply a fine mist of water using a spray, on to the back of the print and leave it to soak in.

The first layers of flat colour are painted on to the matrix, building up a few coats but allowing them to dry to a velvet sheen before more slip is applied.

The paper transfer technique is an ideal process to use on the matrix, and sections of newsprint can be prepared with a variety of colours.

Torn sections of the slipped paper can be applied to the surface, embedding the layers of colour into the surface with a roller.

Step 4: Place a section of the painted newsprint face down on to the surface and use a tool or textured roller on the back of the paper to transfer the colour and create specific marks.

Step 5: Another option is to run a tool, or the end of a paintbrush, over the back of the slipped paper when it is in place, transferring defined marks. The process will leave a pattern on the paper that can be transferred to another section of the block.

Detail can be created in the print transfer by using a textured rolling pin over the back of the paper, transferring specific sections of the slip.

Drawn details can be produced by engraving designs on the back of the slipped paper during the transfer process.

The surface of the clay can be embossed and printed with textures that will be reproduced when printed on to the fabric substrate. Feathers, stencils, wire and textile fragments, in fact a wide variety of different textures, can be embedded into the surface for added detail.

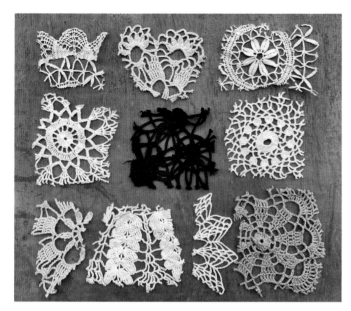

Sections of handmade doilies that have been crocheted in cotton or linen thread, are ideal for making patterns, due to the open-weave designs.

A collection of stencil shapes that consist of a mixture of laser-cut rings and found objects, including spacers used for domestic tiling.

Natural fragments collected on coastal walks, feathers, roots and grasses, all of which can be embedded into the clay to create more organic marks.

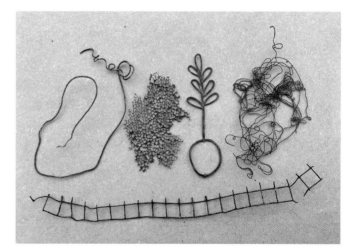

Meandering and twisted wire shapes and a fragment of sea coral can be used in the printing process and will create fine linear markings in the clay.

Applying Colour to the Matrix, Stage 2

This dynamic method of printing offers many ways to apply colour to the matrix and it is a technique that develops as the experiments unfold and new prints are made.

Step 1: A sgraffito comb is another way of transferring details from the slip to the surface, and those that seem to be the most effective are the ones with teeth that are spaced quite wide apart. The result of each transfer can vary as it is dependent on the consistency of the slip and how much has been applied to the paper.

Step 2: Fragments of crochet and a feather can be placed on to the clay for added detail. A roller and a sheet of clean newsprint are used to compress the items into the surface.

Step 3: A section of the slipped newsprint is then placed directly over the inlaid material, using a roller to help transfer the colour, and the paper is then peeled away. Once the fragments are removed from the surface, those areas need to be inlaid with a roller over newsprint as before.

Step 4: The china clay slip can be used to produce a different quality and texture to the marks. It can be dried into small blocks to make colour pastels, using the same process for making colour sticks as described in Chapter 4, and the colour can be adjusted to create a variety of shades. The pastel can be grated using a domestic sieve over an open-weave fabric or stencil on to the clay surface.

Step 5: Mist the slab very lightly with water to soften the pastel, but take care, as too much water will blur the image. Remove the stencil, then inlay the pastel using the roller and newsprint.

Step 6: Another method is to create coloured clay slivers by drying any residue of the slip left in a plastic container. This can be broken up into small fragments that can be sprinkled on to the surface or through stencils, and inlaid into the surface with a roller; it will become printable as the fragments absorb moisture from the clay.

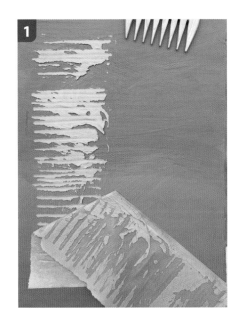

Specific marks can be made in the slip with a sgraffito tool, and the colour left on the paper can be incorporated into the print.

A feather and a fragment of crochet are embedded into the matrix using a roller and newsprint so they are level with the clay surface.

Panels of slipped newsprint have been placed over the embossed pieces, the colour applied, and the paper and items peeled away.

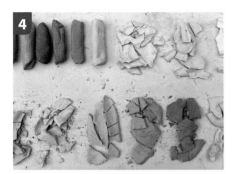

An alternative way to use the china clay slips is to dry them to make slivers; the blocks resemble artist's pastels.

Elaborate detail is achieved by grating colour sticks with a domestic sieve, through commercial stencils, laser-cut leaf shapes and fragments of crochet.

The dried particles of china clay are an alternative to the grated colour, and are sprinkled through a stencil and embedded into the design.

Negative paper stencils can be used with the transfer method, and any residue colour left on the stencil can also be applied on the surface.

The Tyvek stencil is peeled away once the slip has dried a little, to reveal the positive shapes in a bold flat colour.

Another china clay slip is applied in a bright, contrasting colour using the Tyvek stencils, adding graphic detail to the design.

Step 7: Stencils are an ideal option for applying some graphic quality to the process; they can be hand-cut from newsprint or Tyvek paper. Remember to inlay them into the surface before applying any colour. Negative or positive shapes can be used, and it is useful to cut the slipped paper to fit the area that is intended for the transfer, to protect the surface around it. Use a section of the prepared slipped paper and place it on top of the stencil, and use a roller to transfer the colour.

Step 8: The stencil can be peeled away and the colour inlaid into the surface with the roller.

Step 9: Additional graphic detail can be applied over the blocks of flat colour using the Tyvek stencils, as layering images is a significant element of this process.

The pony roller is used to compress the Reemay fabric into the print, working over the whole surface in different directions.

The important factor in achieving a successful print is lightly misting the Reemay print with water at regular intervals.

Using a spoon to burnish the colour into the fabric works well, especially into the corners and edges of the print.

THE PRINTING PROCESS

Make sure that all the slips that have been applied to the clay surface have dried to a dull sheen, and that all fragments of collage, fabric or paper have been removed. Press over the whole slab with a sheet of clean newsprint and a pony roller for the final time, to ensure a level, flat surface ready for printing. To edit the image and create a clean, crisp border to the print, place a strip of drywall tape along each edge. Run each strip through a bowl of water, but then take away the excess water with the fingertips along the whole length of the strip. Press them firmly into place, making sure they are fixed to the clay, as they won't stay attached if pressed on to the wooden frame.

Cut the Reemay fabric to the correct size and mist it lightly with water, making it damp but not too wet, and do the same to the clay. Place the fabric on to the clay, and roll the pony roller over the whole surface, back and forth in different directions, using an even pressure.

Lift one side of the fabric away from the clay, and mist the air just above the slab and the fabric – but avoid spraying directly on to the slab as too much water may cause the print to blur.

Place the fabric back down and compress with the roller again, repeating this action on all four sides. This procedure may have to be repeated several times, so look at the progress of the transfer by peeling one side away and misting with water again if needed, to complete the transfer. It is important to build up the moisture gradually, so light misting and compressing with the roller with a direct and even pressure is the key to a successful print. A spoon can be used to burnish the edges and the corners of the print that the roller can't quite reach.

Once the transfer is complete, the Reemay fabric can be peeled away and laid on to a few sheets of newsprint to dry.

As there is still slip left on the matrix, additional prints can be taken, and these new transfers will reveal different layers of colour. The dimensions of the image to be printed can be changed by taping off a smaller area with the dry-wall tape, or creating a negative stencil with newsprint and pulling a print through that. When printing from a smaller area, rubbing the back of the paper with a burnishing tool or a spoon can help with the transfer of colour. To start again, new layers of slip can be applied over the existing slab – there is no need to clean the original layers of slip or add new clay. Remember to follow the same procedure as before: inlaying each layer of colour as you go with a roller over a sheet of newsprint.

After compressing the image with the roller until a good transfer has been achieved, the print can finally be peeled away from the matrix.

American ceramic artist Mitch Lyons set up his large matrix table for printing on clay in his studio over four decades ago, and it served him well.
(PHOTO: MEREDITH WAKEFIELD)

When the print on the Reemay fabric has dried, the colours will lose some of their vibrancy and they will become matt in appearance. It can be left in this condition, but Mitch Lyons used a water sealant and a soft, flat brush, or sprayed the surface to brighten the colours again. If the sealant is transferred into a water spray, this is the most practical option, as applying a brush may smudge the design.

To store the clay panel, it is important to keep it in a leather-hard condition, and any tape left from printing should be removed. A very damp sheet of newsprint can be placed over the surface and wrapped in plastic. If left too long the paper will start to disintegrate, so replace it regularly.

After twelve years of experimenting with this technique, Mitch Lyons finally felt he had achieved the correct formula of pigments and substrate to produce successful prints. In September 1980 he prepared a large clay slab matrix in his studio that measured 6ft by 6ft (182.88 by 182.88cm), and printed from that same slab until his death in 2018.

CHAPTER 8

THE FIRED SURFACE

Decorating the ceramic surface can be done at every stage of the making, which enables the potter to build a sequence of refined layers to the work. A biscuit-fired surface is porous and can be chalky with an unfinished quality to it. The nature of a harder, resilient surface requires a different approach, using alternative versions of techniques that are not so effective on unfired clay, and will sometimes require different materials to achieve them. There are many ways to enrich the characteristics of a biscuit-fired surface, and there is a diversity of colour and glaze applications.

SMOKE FIRING

The process of sawdust firing is a straightforward method, and most of the firing techniques do not require specialist equipment. It has been developed by contemporary makers from the traditional pit and bonfire kilns used for centuries by potters from all over the world. The technique requires exposing a low-fired clay to smoke and flames, causing the carbon to be trapped and enveloped into the surface of the clay. It can produce dramatic results and beautiful marks, and the element of chance and the unpredictable nature of this process is what potters find so appealing. It is literally painting with smoke and fire. It is also a technique that will produce a great deal of smoke, so a wide-open space outside is required, and it is advisable to be mindful of any environmental restrictions.

WHAT YOU WILL NEED

There is an eclectic selection of decorative applications covered in this chapter, so a diverse list of equipment is required to cover every process. This is to act as a guide, and there are options with certain techniques that require less equipment, yet have the potential to produce dramatic and exciting surfaces.

Equipment
- Metal garden bin
- Smaller metal bucket with lid
- Household bricks
- Metal sheeting
- Old kiln shelves
- Garden shovel
- Biscuit-fired work or test tiles
- Wire brush
- Metal sanding strip

Materials
- Sawdust
- Straw
- Kindling
- Newspaper

- Lighter fuel
- Flame torch ignition lighter
- Salt
- Seaweed
- Oxides and underglaze colours
- Dried fruit peelings and nut shells
- Ceramic saggars
- Saggar glue
- Copper wire or copper scourers
- Wire wool
- Aluminium foil
- Small bag of soft clay
- Paperclay slip
- Sponge stamps
- Paper stencils
- Latex wax
- Copydex glue
- Glaze powder
- Water-based wax
- Small domestic sieve
- Pony roller
- Brushes and sponges
- Ink
- Watercolour pencils
- Graphite sticks or powder
- Shaving foam

◀ 'Articulata' by the author, on location on the Suffolk coast, where driftwood is collected to pack in her custom-made saggars, when firing the work.

A brick kiln has the advantage in that it can be built to any size to accommodate how much work is to be smoke-fired.

'Full Circle', hand-built in grey stoneware and filled with saggar-fired pebbles by the author, using seaweed and copper wire to create the smoky marks.

Most makers will biscuit fire their work before a smoke firing, at around 800–1000°C (1470–1830°F), which is porous enough to absorb the smoke. They will also choose to burnish the clay, which can be done at different stages of the drying process. At the leather-hard stage soft plastic ribs can be used to compress and develop a polished sheen. If the surface is very dry, a generous coating of baby oil is applied, allowing it to sink in; it is then wiped over with a damp paper towel, which lubricates the surface to assist the burnishing process. This can be done with spoons, a smooth pebble or a burnishing tool, and makes the surface very responsive to a smoky atmosphere. However, a more sculptural, textured surface can also be smoke fired.

A metal dustbin, barrel or a brick kiln are often used to fire the work, and they are filled with layers of different qualities of sawdust; but makers will also add straw, newspaper, wood kindling and other combustibles. The work is packed on to a thick bed of sawdust initially, and once all the work is buried completely, the top layer of sawdust is set alight, then covered with a kiln shelf, a sheet of metal or a dustbin lid, and left to smoulder slowly for several hours. A brick box or brick kiln is the most practical solution, as it can be built with loose bricks to any proportions, to accommodate the size and quantity of work to be fired. This can be built directly on the soil or on a layer of bricks or stone slabs. Gaps are left between some of the bricks to allow for the air to circulate.

If a metal dustbin is used for a smoke firing, six to eight holes can be drilled all the way round at the base of the drum, to increase air circulation and aid combustion.

SAGGAR FIRING

Saggars have a long history and were initially made to protect glazed work from the flames, ash and debris in a firing, as the kilns were originally fuelled by wood or coal. Many potters have adapted them from their original use, and the fumes and smoky atmosphere are now trapped inside the saggars so the work can absorb a smoky atmosphere. They are boxes made of clay, often with a lid, and most potters will build their own, in different shapes and sizes, using a sculptural clay body such as crank, which will withstand the thermal shock. They may crack after several firings, but can be bound with wire to hold them together, or patched up with kiln cement or paperclay.

Saggars can also be made from paper, cloth or aluminium foil. These are more fragile, and usually contain just one item, such as a wrapped parcel, and are not fired on their own, but are often stacked together inside a clay saggar, a brick kiln or a barrel firing, or buried in a pit. The biscuit-fired work can be soaked in a saltwater solution for about three to four hours,

'Saggar Beasts' by the author. The creatures were soaked in salty water, dried, then wrapped in wire wool, copper wire and seaweed.

Potters will often make their own saggars out of a sculptural clay body in different shapes to suit the size of the work they are planning to fire.

and when dried and packed in a saggar, the surface will go pink and orange after firing. Too much salt will create a very intense colour, but the surface of the clay can start to disintegrate post firing. For a regular bucket filled with warm water, add about three to four teacups of salt. This process only works well in the saggar and the barrel firing because of the temperature.

Saggars are fired in a gas kiln, in raku kilns, and in some cases, electric kilns. They must all be in an outside location because of the smoke generated, and lids must be sealed completely, especially if using an electric kiln, as the salt content can eat into the elements. The lids can be sealed with soft clay, but this will often break apart during firing. There is a saggar glue recipe that can be piped from a squeezy bottle in combination with PVA glue: apply it round the rim of the saggar and the underside of the lid, and squelch it into place. Another option is to paste strips of newspaper generously painted with liquid paperclay and placed over the section where the lid meets the saggar. It is worth applying at least two layers of paper.

Saggar glue recipe

To fix and seal the lids of the saggars:

China clay	40
Alumina	40
Ball clay	20

Mix with water so it is a thick, creamy consistency. Apply a layer of PVA glue first, from a squeezy container, and trail it along the rim and inside the lid of the saggar. Then trail the saggar glue over the top of the glue and press the lid firmly into place, with more saggar glue added on the outside edge to fill any gaps.

Saggar-fired porcelain with sterling silver and rubber cord, part of the author's 'Tension Visuelle' collection, a range of sculpture to wear. (PHOTO: RICHARD KALINA)

'Meander', one of the author's feather vessels. Subtle marks are created on saggar-fired porcelain and embellished with a swan feather. (PHOTO: RICHARD KALINA)

BARREL FIRING

Another outdoor firing technique uses a metal drum, which can be cut down to make it a more manageable height if required; it can use more wood, alongside sawdust and straw. This firing chamber may reach a higher firing temperature than an open fire or a pit, allowing for additions of colorants and copper wire to create stronger surface colour. However, this will depend on how much wood is added during the process, and how long it burns for. The pieces are stacked as before on a generous bed of sawdust, and as they are placed in the barrel, straw or sawdust is packed in layers around them, then copper carbonate and salt can be sprinkled between the pieces and throughout the layers. Salt is very helpful as it promotes fuming, and potter Eduardo Lazo, who specializes in raku and smoke-firing techniques, has a mixture that consists of a third of copper carbonate and two thirds of salt: he refers to it as 'magic dust'.

The layers of sawdust are built up and the process repeated until all the work has been covered. Wood kindling is piled on top, and lighter fluid can be applied and allowed to soak in, to ensure it gets off to a good start. Once the flames have died down to become hot embers, the top of the barrel is covered and it should continue to burn and smoulder for a few hours; then it can be allowed to cool.

Elliott Denny's Minimalist Style

Elliott Denny is a potter with a graphic design and printmaking background; he produces tableware and sculptural ceramics in a clean, minimalist style. He references forms, tones and surfaces inspired by architectural details, mechanical components and the natural world. He utilizes a range of production methods including throwing, lathe turning, extruding, jolleying and casting. Elliott is interested in historical and modern industrial production techniques, and how they can be used in the contemporary ceramic studio.

He explains the fascination for this experimental firing technique:

> I began working with smoke firing in 2017 for an exhibition where I wanted to use woodworkers' and fellow exhibitors' waste materials to decorate and fire a collection of small vases. As I enjoy the process and the unpredictable results, I have since done an annual smoke firing and run workshops using the technique.

Potter Elliott Denny at his wheel in his sunny studio, turning one of his architecturally inspired vessels.
(PHOTO: ANNA+TAM)

Elliott Denny uses a stoneware body for the smoke firings, and mounts them on a lathe to refine and burnish the surface.

Elliott smoke fires his work in a garden fire bin, which gives the work, he says '...a unique smoky or galaxy-like surface'. The bin is prepared with layers of sawdust and colorant materials, and the biscuit-fired pots are either placed in between the layers, or they are individually packed into aluminium foil saggars with additional colorants and sawdust.

For colour, he uses skins from bananas, avocado and citrus fruits, as well as coffee grounds, seaweed, leaves, various salts, metal shavings and a sprinkling of copper carbonate. A fire

Some of the polished vessels are packed in individual saggars of aluminium foil with a variety of ingredients, colourants and sawdust.

The garden fire bin is packed with the work, layers of sawdust and a final layer of kindling, newspaper and hardwood.

Once alight, the fire is allowed to burn and establish a good temperature, with glowing embers, before it is covered.

To retain the heat, all the holes round the base of the bin are plugged with clay, and it is left to smoulder and cool down.

The next day the work is unearthed from the ashes of the fire, cleaned with soapy water and waxed to highlight the smoky marks.

Each piece will have different marks and colours, dependent on the materials that Elliott has wrapped in each individual parcel.

is built on top of the final layer of sawdust using newspaper, kindling, medium hardwood and then larger hardwood pieces.

It is lit from the newspaper layer and left to burn and then die down; eventually it is covered, and all air holes at the base of the bin are plugged with clay.

The work is unearthed from the ashes the next day, brushed clean, and then washed; it can then be coated with wax and buffed to bring out the smoky detail.

PIT FIRING

Pit firing entails digging a hole or a trench to create a firing chamber below ground. This type of firing has a slower burn, and the temperature will increase more gradually than the firing methods above ground – as there is less air circulating, the heat is kept in longer and is insulated by the soil around the pit. Sloping the walls of the pit can aid the air circulation and the fire can get hotter more quickly. Some potters, however, choose to fire in a variety of locations and a sandy beach is a popular option. The size and scale will depend on the amount of work that is to be fired, but it can be done on a modest scale.

Step 1: As with all the other methods of smoke firing, the pieces are laid out on a bed of sawdust.

Step 2: Additional layers of sawdust, straw and other combustible materials are built up around the pieces, until all the work is covered.

Step 3: If it is too shallow, it may burn too quickly so it should be at least 2ft (60cm) deep. As a guide, there should be about 8in (20.3cm) above the work. Once the layers of sawdust are in place, enough wood and dry branches can be piled on top.

Step 4: The wood is lit with the aid of crumpled newspaper and lighter fluid or fire lighters to get it started. There should be enough wood for it to burn for long enough to create the desired effects, and the fire should be well established before the pit is covered with metal panels.

In all these firing methods, there is an opportunity to experiment with other combustible materials such as seaweed, eggshells, pine cones, nut shells and plant matter, to name but a few. Straw, string and grasses and vermiculite can be soaked in a salty water solution for about three to four hours, using the same measurement for the biscuit-fired work, then thoroughly dried, tied around some of the work, or laid over sections of the pieces as they are packed into the pit. Copper wire can be wound in a single band or in several sections around a surface, and twisted into place with pliers to make sure the wire is taught and in contact with the surface, so it will leave a strong mark.

The pit is lined with a generous layer of sawdust and the work is then bedded down over the top.

Additional layers of sawdust are applied over the work until they are completely covered.

Wood kindling is piled on top as the final layer, with crumpled newspaper to promote good burning conditions.

Once the fire is established more wood can be added, and the pit can be covered and left to burn and smoulder overnight.

'Lacuna' from the Spindle Collection by the author; it was hand-built and fired in sections in a trench-style pit firing.

A saggar-fired, ovoid vessel that has been sealed with Liquid Quartz™, and created by Made OF Australia™ for the world's finest restaurants. (PHOTO: ANNA-MARIE WALLACE)

Another method to make sure the materials are kept on the surface of the work, is to use panels of soft paperclay, which can be quite sticky, and ideal to wrap around in a band, with different ingredients embedded into the surface. Fine swirls from a copper wire scourer, shell fragments, or a sprinkle of salt are very effective and otherwise would be difficult to hold in place.

The results can be quite different, as it is dependent on the materials used, the temperature reached, and the quality of the work's surface. After firing, in all cases, the work pieces should be left to cool completely before they are unpacked, so they can be cleaned and washed to remove any debris from the firing. To bring out all the subtle smoky marks, the work can be warmed up and beeswax polish or Renaissance Wax can be applied with a smooth cotton cloth, allowing it to soak into the surface to highlight any smoky detail.

There is also a product called Liquid Quartz™ from Australia that is a permeating sealer, rendering the surface waterproof, stain resistant and creating a long-lasting barrier. This has been introduced by artist and designer Anna-Marie Wallace, who set up Made OF Australia, which makes unique saggar-fired tableware for Australia's finest restaurants. More details about their work and the techniques that she and her small team use, can be found in the specialist suppliers' section.

FAST FIRING

The fast-firing technique has the most basic approach, it is simple to do, and has immediate results. The smoke is produced by setting light to some crumpled newspaper in a metal bucket and maybe the odd handful of sawdust or straw, then partially covering it with a metal lid and allowing it to burn and smoke for about ten to twenty minutes.

Metal trays and buckets are ideal containers to use for the fast-firing technique, which can produce decorative smoky marks by just using newspaper.

The fast-firing method of creating smoky marks can produce surprisingly sophisticated surfaces, despite this being the most basic method.

Slip resist can be applied with paper stencils, sponge printing and an engraved design, all producing interesting results.

The work can be raised up on a couple of kiln props or a fragment of kiln shelf inside the bucket, so the paper or sawdust can be placed underneath the work as well as around it. This process can be repeated if darker, smoky marks are required. The process can be quite deceptive as it sometimes appears that the smoke has not made much of an impression on the work, but on cleaning the slip away, subtle and painterly smoky marks are revealed. A few experimental firings will help you to discover the amount of carbon and smoke needed for the desired result.

To create a defined pattern, the clay surface can be masked by a clay slip in different ways. A smooth clay slurry will work, but take care with the application, as it may start to flake off if it is too thick. A design can be painted with a brush, printed using sponge stamps, or slip can be applied around a newsprint paper stencil. The slip layer can also be engraved to create linear marks with a pointed tool, which will expose the clay surface to the smoke.

An intricate pattern of masking tape can be applied to act as a resist before painting the slip. When the slip has lost its shine, the tape can be peeled away and then exposed to the smoky chamber of burning newspaper. A rubber-based glue or latex wax can be trailed on to the surface, painted over with slip, and the glue peeled away from the surface, before firing. The slip resist technique may be suitable for lower temperature firings such as in the brick kiln. Saggar and barrel firings, if they are generating a higher temperature, may result in fixing the slip on to the surface so it cannot be removed post firing to reveal the design.

The decorative marks can be quite varied in tone, depending on how long the clay has been exposed to the smoke.

Deirdre Hawthorne: Her Approach to Creating a Surface

Deirdre Hawthorne is a maker who is not afraid to push boundaries and challenge the imperfections of her ceramic structures. Her visceral, instinctive approach to creating a surface provides an emotional charge to the work:

Deirdre Hawthorne has an instinctive approach to creating her surfaces, and revels in the imperfections and fragility of her vessels. (PHOTO: LEON COOLE)

My imagery and voice are rooted in the Irish landscape, in specific places that hold a charge for me – seashores, islands, forests, gardens, houses and city streets. Through my ceramics, I try to convey the layering of marks, physical and emotional, the natural and the unnatural, ancient, fresh, accidental, or purposely inflicted on places and people.

Deirdre's forms are simple, but for most of the pieces the clay is deeply marked, and then saggar fired to create smoke and reduction effects, pushing the clay to its limits. The surface is often imprinted with plants, fabric or Irish lace. Sometimes she pierces the surface rhythmically with tools, tacks, pins and nails. The marks can dent the surface or go right through. At other times she will leave the nails in place, transforming the vessel into something heavier and more extreme. For many pieces she uses simple slips and glazes, but the final colours come from the chemistry of the saggar firing. She explains: 'Many pieces are lost in the firing but the ones that survive are idiosyncratic and unrepeatable, fragile, dark, yet inherently resilient.'

In the past she experimented with recording her environments directly on to the surface of fired clay by using the photographic process of cyanotype. She hand builds her vessels in porcelain, stretching and piercing the surface and then firing them without allowing the clay to vitrify. This fired surface was soaked in cyanotype solutions and kept in the dark. Just before exposing the pot to sunlight, plants and flowers were attached to act as stencils.

Deirdre Hawthorne has experimented with the photographic process cyanotype on porcelain, which resulted in ethereal structures with ghostly marks. (PHOTO: LEON COOLE)

She says:

The exposure could be erratic, at the mercy of the skies, and the plants would blow and shift, creating a sense of a period of time, rather than a decorative silhouette. Each vessel, whether saggar fired, or sun printed, is a one-off, but together they form interrelated groups. Moments of time, memories of a place, of a family, linked together by form and process but set apart by nuance and chance.

WAX-INCISED TECHNIQUE

This technique involves covering the surface of the clay with an even coating of water-based wax resist, incising a design through that layer, then adding pigment into the engraved lines. The waxed surface will resist the colour over the rest of the surface and will burn away when fired, revealing a detailed linear design. This technique is particularly useful if a written text is required, and if using different engraving tools can produce a variety of incised marks and lines. The wax-incised technique seems to work better on a biscuit-fired surface, as it is easier to achieve fine, sharp lines.

However, to be effective it is important that a layer of colour is applied first, before the layer of wax. There needs to be a substantial layer of colour and wax to create a reasonable depth to the engraved design to be able to fill it with colour. This is not necessary when working on leather-hard clay. The wax can be applied on to a bare, leather-hard clay surface, the engraved design is filled with a contrasting slip resembling mishima, the ancient art of inlay. This method is featured in Chapter 4.

The biscuit-fired surface is painted with a generous but even layer of underglaze colour and allowed to dry. This can be done using one colour, or using different blocks or sections of several colours, which can create a loose design, ready for a defined outline. The area is then painted with an even layer of wax resist, using a soft flat brush, and allowed to dry. The design can be scratched through the wax and into the colour to make a linear design or outline with a fine tool, brushing off any burrs of wax with a soft dry brush.

Apply a dark underglaze colour or diluted oxide directly into the lines with a fine brush, to fill the lines with colour, rather than painting across the whole surface. The work will need to be biscuit fired again to burn off the wax if the piece requires glazing.

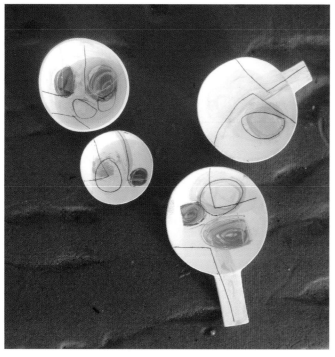

Flat spoon shapes by the author, with painterly layers of underglaze colours over a white background, defined by wax-incised detail.

'Meander Spoon' by the author, a bold layer of yellow with wax-incised squiggles and speckles created by colour residue left on the wax.

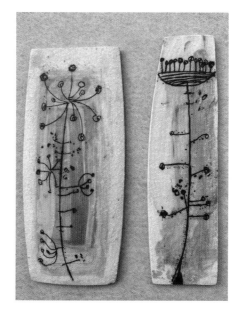

Using a dark underglaze colour or an oxide in the incised wax design, it can resemble fine line drawings or illustrations.

LATEX WAX RESIST

Liquid latex is a material used for prop making and creating flexible moulds, but it can also be used to mask a ceramic surface. It can be applied to leather-hard clay, a biscuit-fired surface, or on to raw glaze, with the opportunity to build up layers of different pigments. As it is a liquid latex rubber, it needs to be peeled off the surface prior to firing. The advantage of using this material rather than wax is that if a mistake is made, it can just be peeled off and started again. Once wax is applied to a surface, it would have to be fired to burn it away. The same process of application will work at whatever stage you choose to use it. It can be trailed, painted and applied through stencils. Tests can be carried out on a biscuit-fired surface, and a catering sauce bottle can be used to trail the latex. The latex can be rinsed out, but if left to set, that should not be a problem as latex can be peeled off most surfaces.

Brushes unfortunately clog up very easily and need to be washed immediately after use. Dipping the brushes in Murphy's oil soap or a laundry stain remover gel prior to use will help to keep them in good working order. Latex can be painted through plastic, paper or vinyl stencils. As soon as the latex is applied, the stencils should be removed immediately to ensure a clean, sharp image, especially if using paper, as this may stick to the surface and cannot be removed in one piece.

After the latex has dried, glaze or colour can be applied over the whole surface, and even though it will coat the latex, this will come away when the layer of latex is peeled off. A needle tool or scalpel can be used to lift an edge of the latex and it

Latex wax and Copydex glue are practical alternatives to use as a resist as they can be peeled away before firing.

will then come away very easily. If the layer of latex is quite generous, it will be much easier to remove.

An alternative to latex wax is Copydex glue, which is a latex-based rubber cement, widely used by model makers and used to bond a variety of materials, including paper, fabric, carpet and wood. A tube of the glue can be converted into a trailer by fixing the tip of a ball-point pen into the lid. A hole is made by heating up a slim metal skewer and inserting it into the lid to make an opening, then a nib can be secured into place with some epoxy resin. The lid can then be screwed back on to the tube, and the glue can be trailed on to a fired surface. A nib can also be glued into a small section of rubber tubing, and this can fit snugly over the top of the tube.

Designs have been trailed, painted and applied through stencils, using latex wax on biscuit-fired tiles, made from different clay bodies.

The designs in latex wax have been peeled away after various matt and textured glazes were applied to the tiles.

The fired results reveal the contrasts between the tone of the clay, the quality of the different glazes, and the marks that can be made by the latex.

GLAZE DUST PRINTS

The dust printing technique featured in Chapter 5 can be adapted to use alternative materials, such as powdered glaze. Glazes that have been mixed with water will work well, as the glaze can be dried out very easily on a cloth over a plaster block, crushed and then refined into a powder using a domestic sieve. If there are powdered glazes on hand that haven't been mixed up with water, they would be ideal to use. The same process for creating the images is the same, and stencils can be used in different ways to guide the design.

The glaze dust that accumulates on the surface of a stencil, for example, can be used to create another print by carefully placing a soft clay slab over the stencil, so as not to disturb the dust and compress it into the clay by using a rolling pin. This should be done on an absorbent surface to prevent the clay from sticking.

The stencils and glaze dust can be applied to the clay surface directly, but using a sheet of newsprint and a roller to compress the dust into place.

To create dust prints on a biscuit-fired surface is tricky, as the dust will sit on top of the surface and tends to slide off. To prevent this, a generous coating of CMC gum can be painted on the tile, immediately before the glaze dust is applied through a stencil, and this will allow it to stick to the surface. However, care should be taken to keep the surface level, and not to disturb the decoration until after it has gone through the glaze firing, which will fix it permanently.

Reiko Miyagi and her Use of Glaze

Reiko has started to explore the delights of glaze, to balance the graphic qualities of her sgraffito work. While she enjoys working with the sgraffito technique, which fulfils her urge to express the images that flood her imagination, sometimes she wishes to make more subtle work that blends into the surroundings or works well to serve food.

To achieve this ambient-toned work, Reiko uses two or three different glazes to paint her designs. She starts by applying the glaze by brush, or uses a ladle to pour it over a section of the piece. Then she covers the same area by brushing on wax resist. After letting the wax dry, a second glaze is applied. Additional colours are made by dipping into the glazes at different angles, and where they overlap, a third colour is formed.

Glaze powder is applied through a stencil with a small sieve, directly on to an absorbent surface, ready to impress with clay.

The glaze dust left on the stencil is kept in place, so an impression can be taken with a soft sheet of clay.

The result of the print is not only a transference of the glaze, but the embossed detail of the stencil outline.

Sections of thin card stencils, with a dusting of glaze powder, are embedded together into the surface with a roller and newsprint.

The result is a textured surface, with the glaze granules still visible and a change of colour to the clay around the edges of the glaze.

The glaze still retains its granular quality after firing, with the potential to vary, depending on the type of glaze and the colour of the clay.

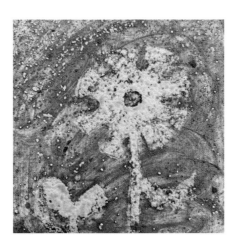

The solution to applying glaze dust to a biscuit-fired surface is a generous coating of CMC gum, allowing the glaze to stay in place.

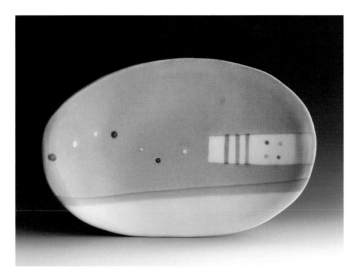

The soft, muted tones of Reiko Miyagi's glaze work are in sharp contrast to the graphic qualities of her sgraffito pieces.

Reiko Miyagi combines two or three different glazes for her ambient-toned work, and uses wax resist to create her designs.

TEXTURED AND EMBOSSED SURFACES

Several of the techniques featured in this book produce embossed, textured and engraved detail in a clay surface, and once they have been biscuit fired, there is an opportunity to enhance that detail in various ways. Washes of oxide, underglaze colour, and an engobe often referred to as a biscuit slip can be painted in combination over the textured surface.

These pigments or contrasting coatings of glaze can be painted into the surface and then wiped away, leaving the pigment in the recesses and revealing all the subtle marks and enhancing the design. Oxides can be diluted with water to mix into a watercolour-like consistency, and it is helpful to add a dash of medium. It will assist in fixing the pigment to the surface, and restricts the possibility of smudges as the water evaporates.

The intensity can be adjusted, and several layers can be applied until the right tone is achieved. These are strong pigments and will stain the surface very easily, and it is often difficult to judge the final outcome, so it is worth testing a range of oxides and familiarizing yourself with the application.

Liquid underglazes are brighter, have a larger range of colours to choose from, and are not as strong as oxides so will not stain the clay surface so easily. They can be used in the same way, painted into cavities and wiped away from the rest of the surface. Several colours can be used over a surface, and like oxides, they can be fired without a glaze. In both cases if a transparent glaze is used, the pigments will intensify in colour and become brighter.

Glazes can be treated like pigments and applied just in the crevices, or painted or poured over the whole surface; they will often pool or break up over the design, which can be very effective. A semi-transparent celadon type of glaze is an ideal candidate to highlight an embossed design, and is popular with makers such as American potter Steve Kelly, as it can produce sophisticated surfaces so easily, especially on embossed porcelain.

Combining several glazes, or applying them over slips or oxides, can produce dramatic results, and it is here that testing is a crucial part of the creative process. The combinations are endless, and it is important to keep careful notes.

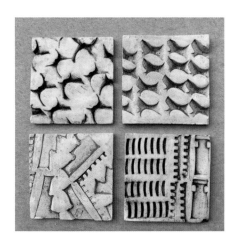

Two different washes of oxide, cobalt oxide and vanadium pentoxide, have been used to enhance the deep recesses created by metal components.

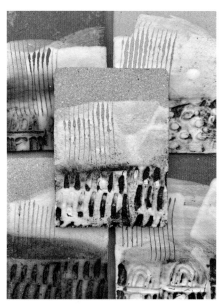

A series of tests using a crackle slip, painted unevenly over oxides that have been inlaid into the embossed prints.

A mixture of cobalt oxide and nickel oxide was applied to fired samples that were embossed with the sculpting medium stamps.

The cobalt oxide and nickel oxide mixture was washed into the engraved detail of the tests, made by hot glue-pen doodles.

The brighter palette of underglaze colours can also be used to highlight embossed detail made by crushed peanut shells.

American potter Steve Kelly uses a semi-transparent glaze over his water-etched porcelain pieces, so they pool beautifully into the recesses.

A collection of tests exploring the possibilities of different glazes, in combination with slips over an embossed design.

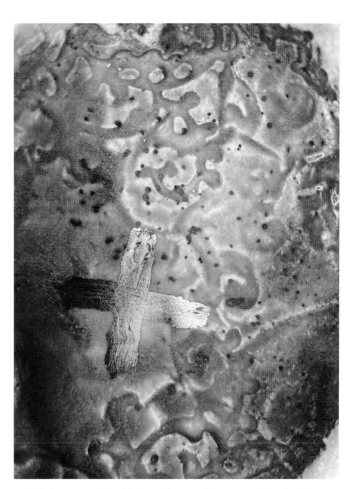

Embellishments can be added post firing, such as copper foil, a detail that helps to enhance the colour of the glaze.

GLAZE APPLICATION

There is a range of textured glazes that are dry in appearance and can also have a crusty or crater-like surface; these work particularly well on sculptural ceramics. They can, however, be an alternative glaze to add highlight to detail with an organic finish to a fired surface.

Glaze can be applied in different ways, though painting, pouring, spraying and dipping are the main methods used by makers. The wax resist technique using sponge stamps can come into play, using glaze instead of underglaze colour. The wax can be applied directly to the biscuit-fired surface with the sponge stamps, or on top of a fresh layer of glaze. The glaze can also be directly printed, taking advantage of the quality and texture that a sponge print will produce.

Glaze can also be spread over the surface with the fingertips or smeared with the palm of the hand, or flicked and splattered in a gestural way.

A sample of a dry textured glaze painted into the surface of a terracotta crank tile that had been embedded with a fine linear seaweed.

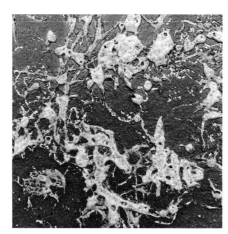

This inlaid texture has been created by a volcanic glaze that bubbles, and has a crater-like appearance, depending on the thickness of the glaze.

A very effective way to produce dramatic results is to print a wax design with a sponge stamp between two different glazes.

The round, float-inspired forms have been used to test a variety of glazes, using elements of printing with stamps and wax resists.

Glaze can be applied with hands or fingertips, producing chaotic marks and varying depths of glaze application.

Hilary Mayo, and her Method of Glazing her Landscape Vessels

Hilary Mayo has developed a specific method to glazing her landscape vessels, involving several stages to the process. She builds up several different layers of glaze to achieve very painterly qualities on her vessels, which have been inspired by the dramatic Icelandic landscape and, more recently, the eroding Suffolk coastline.

Step 1: She starts by painting a dry white glaze over the black underglaze on the outer wall of the vessel. The right consistency of glaze and the application is crucial: the brush needs to be wet, but with no excess water, and it shouldn't be overloaded with glaze. She explains: 'I use a quick, light, criss-cross action so the glaze is blended, with variations in thickness that respond to the surface undulations.'

Step 2: Once this layer is complete, using a sharp knife, she carefully defines the edges of the base, the vertical line of the slab, and her impressed maker's mark.

Step 3: Hilary leaves this glaze layer to dry, and any areas that are too thick are gently sanded.

Hilary Mayo landscape vessels have several layers of slip, glaze and oxides to achieve the quality of a landscape, a sense of place. (PHOTO: ZUZA GRUBECKER)

It is crucial that the layer of dry white glaze is applied correctly and blended over the surface undulations. (PHOTO: ZUZA GRUBECKER)

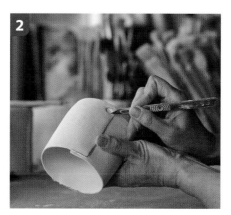

Once the initial glaze layer has dried, Hilary can tidy and refine the details with a sharp knife, taking special care with the edges and rim. (PHOTO: ZUZA GRUBECKER)

Any areas of the glaze that prove to be too thick, Hilary gently rubs with sandpaper to get the variations she requires. (PHOTO: ZUZA GRUBECKER)

Step 4: She then adds patches of a rusty glaze, which is barium based with vanadium; once these are dry, they are gently sanded again.

Step 5: Hilary uses very dry or matt glazes, so she highlights the interior of the vessel with a transparent, shiny glaze, which is also added to the inside of the rim and left to dribble down. Too thick, and it won't dribble and will go cloudy when fired; too thin and it doesn't shine.

Step 6: Finally, Hilary adds trickles of crackle glaze to the outside of the vessel. This is tricky to apply and she uses a flat hake brush, its size dependent on the size of the vessel, a thin,

soft-bristled, rounded brush, with a jug of water at the ready. To achieve the desired crackle, the glaze must be thickly applied, but still with enough fluidity to run down the wall of the vessel. The dry layer of glaze repels the wet glaze, creating the crackles; however, they can begin to peel away, and even fall off.

Step 7: To prevent this, Hilary quickly takes the clean rounded brush, dips it in clean water and gently touches the vessel with the tip of the brush just above the place where the glaze is curling away from the pot. As the water dribbles down the crackle glaze, it is drawn back to the wall of the vessel and becomes attached to the surface again. Hilary must often repeat this process, even when the vessels are in the kiln.

Hilary uses glazes that have a dry, matt quality, and the rusty glaze is used to emphasize the undulations in the forms. (PHOTO: YESHEN VENEMA)

As a contrast to the matt exterior, she highlights the interior of the vessel with a shiny, clear glaze, allowing it to trickle down inside. (PHOTO: ZUZA GRUBECKER)

The crucial element is the glaze trickles on the outside, which are tricky to achieve and can lift away as they dry. (PHOTO: ZUZA GRUBECKER)

Hilary uses a wet paintbrush at the critical moment as the glaze dries, to coax the glaze trickles back into place. (PHOTO: ZUZA GRUBECKER)

A subtle but quietly dynamic vessel by Hilary Mayo using the same glazing process and evoking the same passion for landscape. (PHOTO: YESHEN VENEMA)

FOAM PRINT

This quirky technique uses a layer of shaving foam to transfer underglaze colour to the clay surface. A generous layer of foam is spread out evenly with a straight-edged tool or a rib on to a sheet of plastic, waxed paper or a plastic tray.

Underglaze colour is trickled, trailed or splattered over the surface of the foam, and then a tool or the end of a paintbrush trails into the foam mixture in a meandering fashion, blending the colours slightly.

A biscuit-fired tile or a ceramic form can be pressed or rolled into the mixture, so the foam coats the whole surface and transfers the colour at the same time. The foam is then rinsed away under a running tap. Take care not to touch the decorated

A quirky technique that involves using a generous layer of shaving foam, with underglaze colours trickled on top and swirled together.

The test tiles have been pressed into the mixture of shaving foam and underglaze colour, transferring the design.

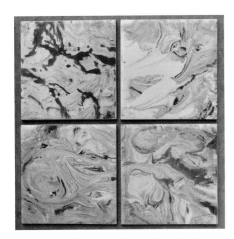

The foam has been rinsed away from the tiles under a running tap and has revealed the swirling, marble effects on the clay.

Underglaze colours have been poured out into a shallow bowl and swirled together to create a pattern in the liquid.

The underglaze colours have been allowed to pool and swirl on to a clay surface, which intensifies the design as the colours blend.

surface as it will smudge, so allow it to dry completely. The result is reminiscent of the method of aqueous surface design, when colour is floated on water for paper marbling.

Underglaze colour can also be marbled directly on to a biscuit-fired surface. The liquid underglaze colour may need to be diluted slightly with water, to make sure the colours are all the same consistency; it should be fluid enough to be able to move over the surface of the clay. The colours are poured into a shallow bowl first, swirled and blended slightly, mixing them into a defined pattern.

The underglaze mixture is poured on to the clay, the ceramic piece is moved and tilted to allow the colours to spread and pool over the surface, and extra movements will adjust and cajole the colour into a more complex pattern. The colours are then allowed to dry, and if a transparent glaze is required, the work would benefit from a biscuit firing first, as the layer of underglaze colour is quite thick and a firing will make it easier to glaze.

SCRATCHED SURFACE

The ceramic surface can be distressed by scratching and engraving at different stages of the making process, but it can work well at the biscuit stage as the clay is still soft enough to make defined marks. The scratches can be done through layers of colour, slip or glaze, and with different tools. Wire brushes, metal skewers and a copper metal scourer are among the options that can create a scratchy surface. Scottish potter

Wendy Kershaw, who works with porcelain, uses a metal sanding mesh, creating subtle and delicate marks on her surfaces; details of her process can be found in Chapter 5. Different clay bodies will yield different characteristics in the marks, and these can be emphasized with washes of colour. This method can be combined with other techniques – for example, using transferred slip prints as a background.

The samples show the quality of lines and marks that can be achieved by scratching the surface on different clays, and how varied it can be.

'Patera', from the author's Gradus Collection, using a wire brush to make the marks through a layer of engobe. (PHOTO: RICHARD KALINA)

Laser-cut vinyl stencils have been applied to a biscuit-fired surface that has been printed with detail using a panel of silk-screen film.

A contrasting underglaze colour has been painted over the whole surface of the tile, using several coats to achieve an opaque layer.

The vinyl has been peeled away and the intensity of the orange underglaze has increased after the firing, highlighting the graphic detail.

VINYL STENCILS

Vinyl is the ideal material to make stencils for a biscuit-fired surface as they will stick very easily to the fired clay. This is because they have an adhesive surface on one side once the backing layer has been peeled away. The designs can be digitally cut, or hand-cut with scissors or with a scalpel, and work well with underglaze colours or oxides; they can also be used to create patterns with glaze. If the stencil is cut out from the vinyl sheet, leave some background around the shape, to hold it together – when the backing paper is peeled away, leave the background intact and apply the whole piece to the biscuit-fired surface. Once in place, it is easier to then peel away the background pieces with the help of a sharp knife, which can anchor the stencil shape in place during the process. The stencils then can be pressed down on to the surface, using a rib to make sure the edges are firmly in place.

Once the colour or glaze has been applied and it has been allowed to dry, the stencils can be peeled away to reveal the patterns ready for firing.

ALTERNATIVE MATERIALS

There are other materials that do not require firing and can be used as an alternative to using a glaze or ceramic colours. Ink is a medium that has always appealed to makers, and will soak into a smooth and porous biscuit-fired surface quite easily.

To get the best results, it is important that time is taken to sand the clay with wet-and-dry sandpaper to achieve a silky smooth surface. Several layers can be applied using coloured inks, which can lead to a dramatic colour. A beeswax or Renaissance wax can be used to seal and create a sheen to the surface.

A smooth surface is crucial for another unconventional material to work well: watercolour pencils can be used to draw and scribble a design over a biscuit-fired surface. A wax coating, as before, can seal the coloured pencil and prevent it from smudging.

Graphite is another material with the potential to provide an intriguing patina. It is available in sticks or powder form, and can create a rich, dark surface on a biscuit-fired surface – the key is that it is porous enough so that it can be absorbed. The graphite sticks come in a wide range of grades and resemble a chunky crayon. Some are water soluble, which can produce beautiful tones and depth. After application, the surface can be polished and buffed with soft cloth to create a subtle sheen. These alternative finishes could also be treated with Liquid Quartz™ to seal the surface and help retain their qualities.

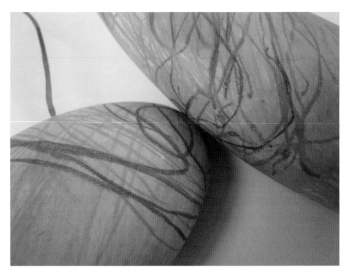

Meandering scribbles made by watercolour pencils are surprisingly effective on a smooth, white, ceramic surface.

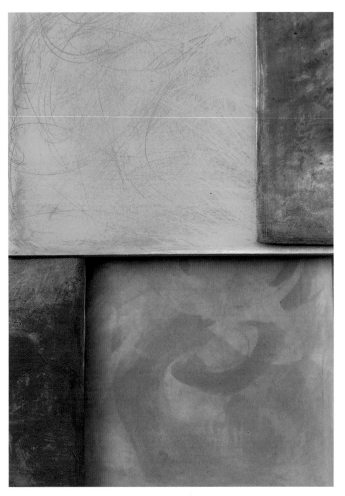

Ink is a reliable and dynamic alternative to ceramic pigments and can produce an interesting patina to a biscuit-fired surface.

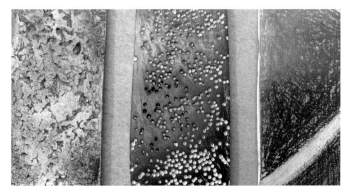

Graphite seems an appropriate choice as it can generate a dark, metallic and polished finish to a smooth or embossed clay.

A collection of Sarah Rayner's delicate, porcelain pods. They are imaginary but have elements that are familiar. They reveal hidden details and tiny decorative crevices. (PHOTO: GREG PIPER)

This sculptural piece by the author, 'Tumulus,' has combined a saggar fired form with a porcelain paper clay cast of a seedpod, embellished with a layer of patinated copper leaf.